Birdwatching walks
in the Lake District

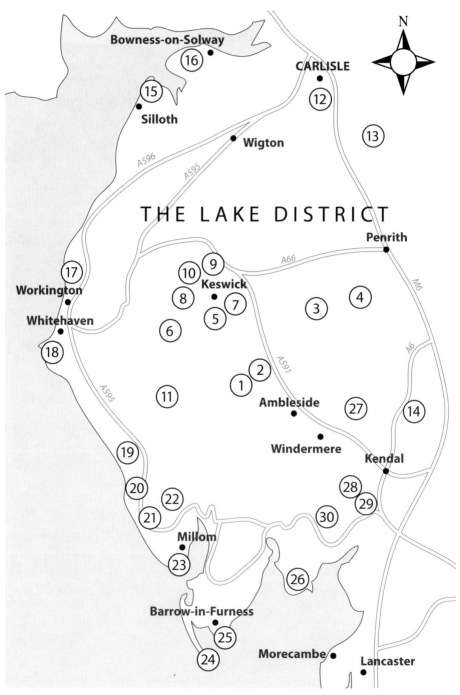

Area map showing walk locations

Bowness-on-Solway

16

CARLISLE

15

12

Silloth

13

A596

A595

Wigton

THE LAKE DISTRICT

Penrith

A66

17

9

10

Keswick

4

Workington

8

7

3

Whitehaven

5

A591

18

6

2

A595

11

1

Ambleside

27

14

19

Windermere

20

Kendal

22

28

21

30

29

Millom

23

26

Barrow-in-Furness

25

24

Morecambe

Lancaster

N

Birdwatching walks
in the Lake District

David Hindle MA and John Wilson BEM, MSc.

Palatine Books

Copyright © David Hindle and John Wilson

First published in the UK in 2010 by
Palatine Books
an imprint of Carnegie Publishing Ltd,
Carnegie House,
Chatsworth Road,
Lancaster LA1 4SL
www.palatinebooks.com

Cataloguing-in-Publication data
A catalogue record for this book is available from the British Library

ISBN 978-1-874181-67-5
Typeset by Carnegie Book Production, Lancaster
Printed and bound in the UK by Jellyfish Solutions Ltd

Contents

Introduction

THE ENGLISH LAKE DISTRICT is justifiably one of the most popular areas in the country and visitors from all over the world enjoy its wonderful beauty throughout the ever-changing seasons. Set against a background of mountains, lakes, woodlands, rivers, picturesque villages and generally fantastic scenery there is much wildlife to delight the visitor.

The area covered in this guide includes the central Lake District National Park and the peripheral areas of the Eden Valley and the Cumbrian coast. The latter includes the Cumbrian parts of both the Solway Coast AONB and Morecambe Bay. Within these boundaries there are many centres of ornithological and wildlife excellence, and taken as a whole the area covered by this book is indisputably a great region in which to explore and enjoy a wonderful hobby.

Each of the manageable walks in this brand new book is intended to provide an introduction to the birds of this unique area, for beginners and expert alike. The walks have been chosen carefully, and where appropriate information on bird identification, habitat, song, conservation issues, and general background information have been incorporated. The book is designed specifically to stimulate interest in bird watching, but also to maximise enjoyment of the walks we also include occasional references to other wildlife and items of cultural and historical interest.

The Lake District has many literary associations including Wordsworth, Keats, Coleridge, Ruskin and Beatrix Potter, most of whom seem to have been inspired by the local wildlife. Indeed it was the original bard of Lakeland, William Wordsworth, whose philosophy was perhaps a forerunner of the National Trust ideology. As early as 1810 William mused over the idea of the lakes as a conservation area, referring to it as 'a sort of national property in which every man has a right and interest who has an eye to perceive and a heart to enjoy'. Today the National Trust, founded in 1885, owns and manages vast areas of the Lake District; one of its first acquisitions was Brandlehow Wood on the edge of Derwentwater in 1902. We have to thank Beatrix Potter for having had the foresight to use the royalties from her books to purchase properties and huge acres of land to protect her beloved Lakeland. Following her death in 1943, she bequeathed 4,000 acres of land to the National Trust.

Twentieth-century developments in 1951 first saw the formation of the Lake District National Park to protect the landscape and its wildlife through unified planning control. It is this area within the park's boundaries that is generally regarded as the Lake District or, perhaps more affectionately, Lakeland. As an entity the park is situated entirely in the county of Cumbria, is roughly circular and about thirty miles in diameter. In addition to the park Cumbria has more Sites of Special Scientific Interest (SSSI) than any other county in England and, not surprisingly, the largely unspoilt countryside offers a rich biodiversity and is a haven for wildlife and birds in particular. For example, the RSPB manages five important reserves in the county at Hodbarrow, Millom, St. Bees, Campfield Marsh and Haweswater. Within the county there are also many other nature reserves, run by different organisations, including Natural England and the Cumbria Wildlife Trust. Since 2000, ospreys have successfully bred in Lakeland and become a major tourist attraction in their own right. There are excellent facilities for viewing the nest site in Dodd Wood, Bassenthwaite, and via a CCTV facility at the Whinlatter Visitor Centre.

It must be emphasised that the bird watching notes serve only as a guide to the species that may be encountered on a particular walk. We cannot, of course, guarantee that you will see most of the birds at every location but we hope that by visiting the correct recommended habitats at the right time of the year your chances will be maximised. The time of year is, of course, very important. For example, the period March to June is the prime time for resident breeding birds, with late April to June the optimum period for summer migrants. Coastal waders and wildfowl are largely present from late July to late May. However, with bird watching there is always an element of pure chance in finding something good and inevitably there will be certain species that the watcher will come across that we have omitted to mention.

For many years members of the Cumbria Bird Club have extensively studied the bird life of Cumbria. To date, three atlases covering the distribution of breeding birds in Cumbria have been completed and a fourth is being researched at the time of writing. These studies have revealed many changes over a period of time and where appropriate we have drawn upon this and other sources of reference in order to update the present status of Cumbria's breeding birds.* Perhaps not surprisingly, there are both losses and gains. Climate change and increasing human pressures in wintering areas in sub-Saharan Africa are thought to be mainly responsible for the precipitous decline of many of our summer visitors, including cuckoo, whinchat, ring ouzel, spotted flycatcher and wood warbler. The changing pattern of farming, particularly in the lowland areas of Cumbria, has led to declines in many birds, especially lapwing, yellow wagtail, yellowhammer and skylark.

---

* Readers of this book can help in further assessing the changes in bird populations by reporting sightings to the Cumbria Bird Club (details on page xi).

Fortunately, diminishing bird populations in Lakeland can be balanced with some gains over the last few decades. It would seem that global warming has led to the expansion of little egret and avocet from southern climes onto the coastal marshes and estuaries of Morecambe Bay, together with restricted numbers of the rare honey buzzard into Lakeland.

During the early 1960s both the peregrine falcon and sparrowhawk were in dire straits and populations almost collapsed owing to the widespread use of three types of organochlorine pesticides used in agriculture. Since restrictions on their use were introduced, beginning in 1962, the populations of these two species in particular have bounced back both nationally and locally. Both of these superb raptors are now regularly seen throughout Lakeland, including the most urbanised areas of Cumbria. Generally, a more enlightened view of predatory birds in recent years has also led to increases in the spread of buzzards, peregrines and ravens, and of course the dramatic colonisation by the osprey.

The large coniferous forests planted by the Forestry Commission now attract more coal tit, goldcrest and increased numbers of crossbill and siskin. Many other woodland and garden birds have also increased at the same time, especially the nuthatch which has dramatically spread from a handful of pairs 50 years ago to the common woodland species that it is today. Elsewhere in Lakeland the recent run of mild winters has resulted in a marked increase of the stonechat.

Before setting out to watch and enjoy the birds of the area, there are certain important points that must be considered.

The use of public transport

Take as long as you need to complete the walks. A leisurely approach is to be recommended; inevitably, therefore, the times and distances given are approximate. The use of public transport provides a greater freedom to complete linear walks and these days is considered to be a more environmentally conscious and a sustainable way of travel, not least because it reduces the chronic traffic congestion that blights the area. Therefore it is recommended that for certain walks indicated by the letters PT local bus and/or train services are utilised wherever possible. Parking facilities are provided near most railway stations and advice regarding the location of bus stops should be sought at the planning stage.

National Rail enquiries: 08457 48 49 50
Traveline (bus enquiries): 0871 200 22 33

Navigation and personal safety

The general walk directions are shown in bold type together with an appropriate symbol and maps are provided as a quick and easy reference. However, we recommend that the appropriate Ordnance Survey Explorer two and a half inches to one mile series of maps be carried on the walks. In particular all of the described walks embracing the Lake District National Park and peripheral areas are covered by Landranger map nos 303, 314, 315 and OL map nos, 4, 5, 6 and 7.

Mountain and fell walks may require navigational skills and the following considerations are essential. While exploring upland areas always carry suitable warm clothing, strong boots, water proofs, plenty of sustenance, a first aid kit and a GPS or a compass. Remember also that there are several areas without clear mobile phone signals. Avoid the fells if there is a likelihood of mist descending or bad weather, which can apply even on a fine summer's day without warning. Always notify someone as to where you are going and when you intend to return. Naturally, the time taken to complete a walk is only approximate and will vary according to factors such as ability, weather stoppages and time spent bird watching.

In coastal areas always consult the tide tables before setting out and beware of rapidly advancing tides and quicksand. Do not wander out onto the intertidal area or away from paths on the salt marshes.

Facilities for the disabled

Unfortunately owing to the wild terrain of Lakeland there is only disabled access to parts of the following walks: 12, 15, 16, 17 and 23.

The countryside code

Naturally the countryside codes should be strictly observed, namely: drop no litter, close all gates, do not damage walls or fences, or in any way disturb stock, avoid all fire risks, and remember it is now unlawful to dig up or pick many species of wildflowers.

Be safe – plan ahead and follow any signs
Leave gates and property as you find them
Protect plants and animals and take your litter home
Consider other people
Keep your dog under close control

Tourist Information

The following list of tourist information offices may prove useful when planning a bird watching holiday in Lakeland. During opening hours details of accommodation, local transport, nature trails and other items of interest can be obtained.

Ambleside, Market Cross, 015394 31576
Borrowdale, Seatoller Barn, 017687 77294
Broughton-in-Furness, The Square, 01229 716115
Cockermouth, Town Hall, 01900 822634
Coniston, Ruskin Avenue, 015394 41533
Grasmere, Red Bank Road, 015394 35245
Kendal, Town Hall, 01539 725758
Keswick, Moot Hall, 017687 72803
Millom, 01229 774819
Penrith, Middlegate, 01768 867466
Whitehaven, 01229 774819
Windermere, 015394 46499

Acknowledgements

It is a pleasure to acknowledge the help given by Christine Dodding and Nicola Breaks for their artistry, and to Mike Malpass, Peter Smith and Stan Craig for providing excellent photographs. Thanks also to Gordon Clarke of Kendal for help with the walk over Helsington Barrows.

Further reading

Birds of Morecambe Bay, Wilson, Dalesman Books (1988)
The Breeding Birds of Cumbria, Stott *et al.*, Cumbria Bird Club (2002)
Birdwatching walks in Cumbria, Dean and Roberts, Carnegie Publishing (2002)
Birdwatching walks in Bowland, Hindle and Wilson, Palatine Books (2007)
Birdwatching walks around Morecambe Bay, Wilson and Hindle, Palatine Books (2007)
The Lakeland Osprey Project, Ramshaw, Lake District Osprey Project (2002)
Birdwatching in the Solway Coast AONB, Irving, Solway Coast Discovery Centre (2008)
Solway Coast Rambles, Irving, Solway Coast Discovery Centre (2008)

The latter two books are available at the Solway Coast Discovery Centre in Silloth.

Sources of useful information

The Cumbrian Bird Report is published annually and covers the status of birds in the county. Up to date information can be obtained by visiting the following websites:

www.cumbriabirdclub.org.uk, for Cumbria Bird Club
www.walneybo.blogspot.com, for South Walney sightings
www.cumbriawildlifetrust.org.uk, Cumbria Wildlife Trust
www.rspb.org.uk/reserves, RSPB reserve information

The Cumbria Bird Club encourages everyone to submit records of sightings at any time of the year. Records can be submitted either electronically or on record cards, which are available from regional recorders. See below for telephone contacts, which are correct at the time of writing but please refer to the website above for the latest contact information.

Barrow and south Lakeland, 01539 727523
Carlisle and Eden, 01228 561684
Allerdale and Copeland, 01946 691370

Disclaimer

The authors have walked and researched the routes for the purposes of this guide. However, while every effort has been made to represent the routes accurately, neither the authors nor the publisher can accept any responsibility in connection with any trespass, loss or injury arising from walking the definitive route or any associated route. Changes may occur in the landscape which may affect the information in this book and the authors and publisher would very much welcome notification of any such changes. That said, we sincerely hope that the walks provide many hours of enjoyable bird watching.

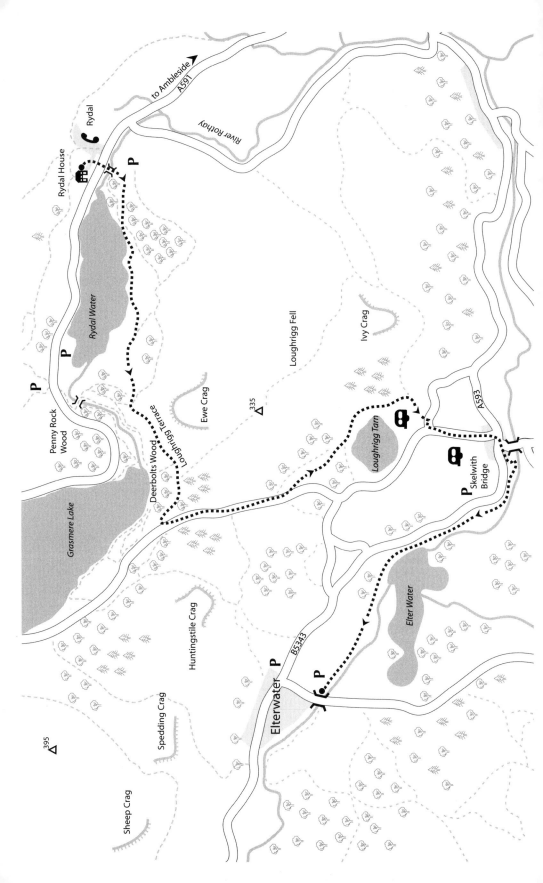

to Ambleside

A591

Rydal

Rydal House

River Rothay

Rydal Water

Penny Rock
Wood

Loughrigg Fell

Ivy Crag

Grasmere Lake

Deerbolts Wood

Loughrigg Terrace

Ewe Crag

335

Loughrigg Tarn

Skelwith
Bridge

A593

Huntingstile Crag

Spedding Crag

Sheep Crag

395

Elter Water

Elterwater

B5343

WALK ONE

Rydal to Elterwater

Heron

Wordsworth's Lakeland

Start: Rydal Mount, Rydal
Finish: Britannia Inn, Elterwater
Grid Ref: NY367067
Distance: 4.3 miles (6.9 km)
Time: Allow four hours
Grade: Easy
General: Refreshment and toilet facilities at Elterwater
village; parking facilities at Rydal (PT). A convenient
bus service links Ambleside with Rydal, and at
Elterwater an hourly bus service departs from
outside the Britannia Inn to Ambleside

THIS LOVELY WALK IN the heart of Wordsworth country embraces three lakes, a tarn, two fast-flowing rivers, and woodland and open areas. Over the ages man has shaped the landscape to suit his needs. He has felled woods, drained marshes and created deserts of agricultural land so that in most areas of England the landscape is only a poor compromise between man and nature. On this walk, however, and throughout the Lake District National Park, the landscape has not undergone radical transformation since William and Dorothy Wordsworth trudged along the shores of Rydal and Grasmere, over three centuries ago.

We commence our walk at Rydal Mount, where in 1813 William Wordsworth moved from Dove Cottage to live out the rest of his life with his family until his death in 1850. Nearby at St Mary's Church it is worth a slight detour in March and April to take in the wooded walk through Dora's Field to admire the wild daffodils. **William and his wife Mary planted the daffodils in memory of their daughter, Dora, who died of tuberculosis in 1847. The daffodils on the gentle slope had nothing to do with the famous poem, though they certainly herald springtime, which is also the best time to capitalise on the ornithological highlights of this walk.**

🚶 **From Rydal Hall/Church cross over the A591 and descend stone steps to cross over the wooden footbridge spanning the River Rothay. Follow a well-defined footpath through woodland alongside Rydal water that opens up to reveal good views across the lake to Rydal Fell. At the south-west end of the lake the footpath ascends along the lower slope of Loughrigg Terrace. Thereafter the footpath enters woodland to reach a metalled road. Turn left and follow the road towards Loughrigg Tarn.**

❶ Resident grey wagtail and dipper haunt the fast-flowing River Rothay and grey wagtail may also be seen on the shore edge of both Rydal Water and Grasmere lake, together with summering common sandpiper. Depending on the season, both lakes harbour small rafts of pochard, tufted duck, goldeneye, goosander, mallard, coot, and larger flocks of Canada and greylag geese. Mute swans are regular and whooper swans are occasional in winter. Kingfisher may add extra sparkle here and is often first located by its high-pitched 'zeeee' call as it flies low over the water.

Ascending onto Loughrigg Terrace and Red Bank there are a number of seats. This is undoubtedly a good place to have lunch while taking in the splendour of Rydal and Grasmere set against the backcloth of the mountains. Continue to enjoy the superb views while walking along the aptly named Red Bank, so called because of the autumnal tints that coat the bracken-covered slope. Above the River Rothay, viewing the serenity of the two lakes below, this must qualify as one of the finest hilltop vantage points in Britain. The plaintive mewing calls of a couple of buzzards soaring on circular thermals above the imposing Rydal Fell might just add the finishing touches. Do not expect to see anything too exotic, although to the north of Grasmere the summit of Helm Crag is dominated by the well-known rocky feature said to resemble a lion and a lamb. Here also be dragons: in particular the attractive golden-ringed dragonfly (*cordulegaster boltonii*) that may be found in rivulets or completely away from water perching on the bracken fronds.

🚶 **Take a left fork along a track and follow waymarkers to the edge**

of Loughrigg Tarn before regaining the main track. Turn right and continue via the hamlet of Tarn Foot, to reach a minor road that links Loughrigg Tarn with Skelwith Bridge.

🛈 En route to Loughrigg Tarn the diverse woodland habitat is interspersed with open areas, providing several opportunities to observe willow warbler, chiffchaff, blackcap, garden warbler, pied flycatcher, redstart and tree pipit. As is usually the case their song provides the first clue as to their whereabouts. The crow family is well represented, with carrion crow, jackdaw and the largest member of the family, the raven. In stark contrast to the raven the most colourful member of the crow family is the jay. Listen for its raucous call and watch for the white rump and sandy brown plumage. Your initial reaction should be to say 'jay,' for usually that is all that is seen of this rather shy species as it flies off into the wood. In the more open areas you may hear the distinctive call of the green woodpecker as it alights on a trunk. This is often described as a laugh, from which this species gets its alternative name of 'yaffle.' This large green and yellow woodpecker topped with a red crown is well worth seeing before it flies off with a bounding flight and yellow rump to the next tree.

Loughrigg Tarn is yet another Lakeland gem. The tranquil water here attracts great-crested and little grebe, mallard, goosander, coot, waterhen and winter diving ducks such as the goldeneye. Any apparent lack of birds on the water may be compensated for by the progressively unfolding view of the Langdale Pikes which dominates this classic viewpoint across Loughrigg tarn, and which is surely one of the most stunning views of mountain vistas to be seen anywhere in England. In the woodland fringe treecreeper, nuthatch, goldcrest and that highlight of a summer visitor, the redstart, with its quivering red tail, may well be spotted. Another animal with a red tail, the red squirrel, used to be present in good numbers in Neaum Wood between Loughrigg and Skelwith but unfortunately now seems to have been displaced by the grey squirrel. As we now know only too well the march of the alien grey squirrel seems relentless and the reds no longer occupy many suitable woods in southern Lakeland.

🚶 **At Skelwith cross over the car park at Chester's by the River Café to gain a bridleway that initially passes several commercial premises before running parallel to the picturesque River Brathay, past Skelwith Force and Eltermere to the village of Elterwater.**

🛈 The walk along the northern bank of the swift-flowing River Brathay is likely to attract grey and pied wagtail and dipper. Tree foliage along the river harbours lesser redpolls, siskin, chaffinch and nuthatch. Another attractive feature of this section of the walk is that it is enhanced by a sudden and dramatic view of the cascading fifteen-foot high Skelwith Force. Further along the Brathay at the confluence of the tranquil waters of Elterwater, the skyline is dominated by the Langdale Pikes in all their splendour. Savour this memorable viewpoint of the lake while checking the water for wildfowl because elsewhere the lakeshore is inaccessible.

On arrival at Elterwater, scan the lake for typical birds of river and lake including mallard, tufted duck, pochard, coot, moorhen little grebe and mute swan. Several species of diving ducks are usually present on the lake in winter, typically represented by goosander, goldeneye and, if luck prevails, an unexpected smew or slavonian grebe. The name Elterwater originates from the Norse 'Elpt Vatn', meaning swan lake, so perhaps the Vikings were familiar with flocks of wintering whooper swans. What is known is that throughout the 1960s and 1970s flocks of up to thirty whooper swans were regular winter visitors to suitable lakes, especially Rydal Water, Grasmere, Elterwater and Bassenthwaite, but today they are no longer common in their former Lakeland haunts.

A possible explanation is that they are particularly well fed at both Caerlaverock and Martin Mere Wildfowl and Wetland Trust centres, which are not too far away as the whooper swan flies. Indeed it is the early birds arriving back from Iceland that catch the piles of grain and potatoes that are left to attract and sustain them throughout the winter. Therefore who can blame the swans for changing their allegiance!

Rydal and Grasmere

Goodsander

Start: Rydal car park
Grid Ref: NY365059
Distance: 4.6 miles (7.4 km)
Grade: Easy
General: Toilets at White Moss car park, refreshments in
Rydal and Grasmere (PT)

THIS WALK, SET IN some of the most glorious Lakeland scenery, offers interesting bird watching throughout the year. The range of habitats include
woodland, fells, lakeshore, fast-flowing streams and marsh. Because of the
excellent range of paths leading from the two car parks situated at either end
of Rydal water, circular walks of several lengths are possible. Spring is best
for the woodland and fellside, while the wetland areas are best in winter.

**The described circular walk starts at the car park at Pelter
Bridge to the east of Rydal Water but it can also be easily
accessed from the much larger car park at White Moss. However,
if this starting point is chosen it is best to do the walk in reverse
going towards Grasmere lake first. From the Rydal car park
proceed along the track past a row of cottages towards Rydal.**

The mature woodland here has breeding pied flycatchers and redstarts.
A good range of resident birds can be seen and heard from the walled
track, including nuthatch, jay, great spotted and green woodpeckers.
However as the return route passes through the wood and there is
more easily watched woodland to come, it is probably best not to
spend too much time searching for these species at this point.

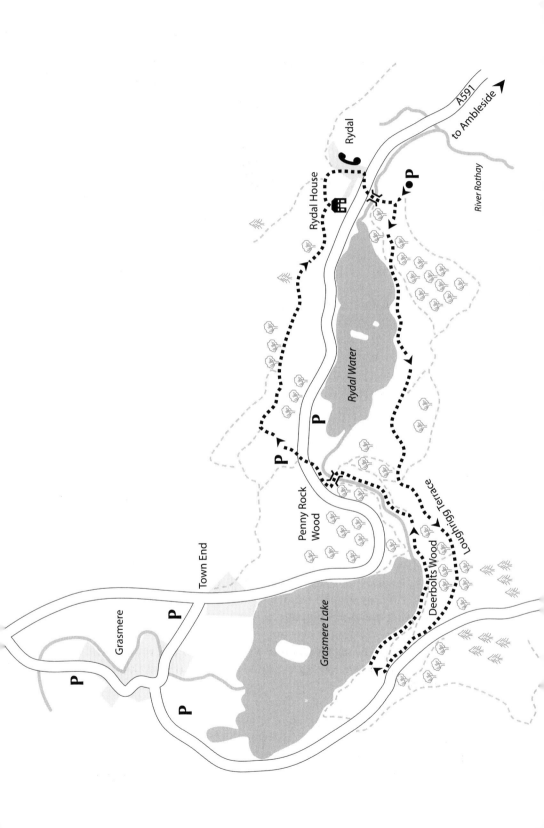

🚶 **Emerging from the woods the elevated position gives excellent views across Rydal Water, with its small islands and rocky outcrops and grassland edge on the far side of the lake. The path passes along the edge of the lake then strikes up the hill towards Grasmere.**

ℹ Breeding birds on the lake include Canada and greylag geese, tufted duck and occasionally great-crested grebe. In winter these are joined by numbers of goldeneye, tufted duck, pochard and goosander. The rocky islands are well used by cormorants, gulls and grey herons. The resident geese regularly graze on the far side of the lake.

🚶 **Follow the signs to Grasmere along the wall of White Moss Wood until you reach the high point and the first sight of a small part of Grasmere comes into view. Take the left-hand path up onto Loughrigg Fell and towards the National Trust's Deerbolts Wood.**

ℹ The bracken-covered hillside with scattered hawthorn, birch and rowan trees attracts breeding tree pipit, wheatear and stonechat and the chance of seeing the declining yellowhammer. Redstarts and spotted flycatchers often sing from the trees towards the edge of the wood. Where there is thicker bushy cover look out for breeding whitethroats and willow warblers. This is a good area to watch for buzzards, peregrine and ravens by scanning the crags and fellsides. There are several strategically placed seats, ideal for watching for raptors overhead and for scanning the bracken and scrub for passerines. Kestrels can regularly be seen hovering over the hillside. In autumn and early winter in a good berry year it is well worth watching any rowan tree full of berries. Thrushes usually feast on these berries first and can include redwing, fieldfare and mistle thrush. The latter regularly tries to stake out a territory and attempts to drive off, with some success, other diners. Later in the autumn and winter the birds turn to the usually more abundant hawthorn berries.

🚶 **Follow the path through the wood and out onto the road for a short distance before taking a public footpath (right) that leads to the lakeshore.**

ℹ In spring pied flycatchers are the star attraction within the mature oak/beech woods which have little or no undergrowth. This trim summer visitor is easiest to find in late April and early May as the males advertise themselves by singing, often from a dead branch close to a nest hole, then intermittently visiting the hole to claim ownership. During much of June they can be seen busily feeding their young in their chosen nest site, but once the young fledge they become very difficult to see as they frequent the tree tops. Other breeding birds include green and great spotted woodpeckers, marsh tit, goldcrest, treecreeper and nuthatch. Wood warblers used to occur in all the woodlands here but numbers are now much reduced so they are not a certainty. Further down the track the woodland has more undergrowth and some clearings ideal for blackcap and garden warbler.

In winter the woods are at their best in years of a good beech mast crop. The path is ideal for watching the ground as tits, nuthatches and finches search among the many leaves for the fallen fruits. Brambling usually occur at such times – look out for their distinctive white rumps as they take flight along with the more familiar chaffinches, They quickly return to the ground and allow you to admire their bright colours. Deerbolts Wood is aptly named, for roe deer are regularly seen and, being so used to humans, they are amazingly easy to observe. The walk along the road passes several large gardens and in winter the number of birds in evidence shows just how important feeding stations at this time of year are. Nuthatches are especially abundant and easily located by their incessant and far-carrying call.

🚶 **Proceed along the lakeshore path back towards Rydal, then cross over the bridge just past the lake weir into Penny Rock Wood, on through the wood and adjoining meadow and into White Moss Common car park**

ℹ️ Grasmere has similar breeding birds to Rydal but it attracts larger numbers of wildfowl in winter, especially at the shallow end towards Grasmere village. Numbers of pochard, tufted duck, goosander and goldenye are regular, along with coot and Canada and greylag geese. Mute swans and mallard patrol the shore touting for tit-bits, but check groups of swans further out, for whooper swans regularly occur. The breakwater over which the exit stream flows is a regular haunt of dipper and grey wagtail and is best viewed from the bridge; also check downstream here and at other locations where the stream is visible as you go through the wood and into the meadow. Penny Rock Wood has similar birds to Deerbolts Wood, although at the right time of year pied flycatchers are even easier to find and approach as they are very used to people. Being mainly oak, the wood lacks the large concentration of birds feeding on beech mast in winter but jays prefer the larger acorns of the oak.

Ⓧ **Leave the meadow and follow the path past the toilets and across the road to the upper car park. Take the path from the car park into the woods and follow the track signposted Rydal. Follow this path to the road by Rydal Mount, turn right at the road then right again at the A591. Take the path opposite the Badger Bar, across the bridge and up through the meadow and wood to rejoin the outward track and then left to the car park.**

ⓘ The woodland birds are very similar to those of the other woods. The more open areas and woodland edges are good for spotted flycatcher and tree pipit. The bridge across the River Rothay gives a further opportunity to look for dipper and grey wagtail.

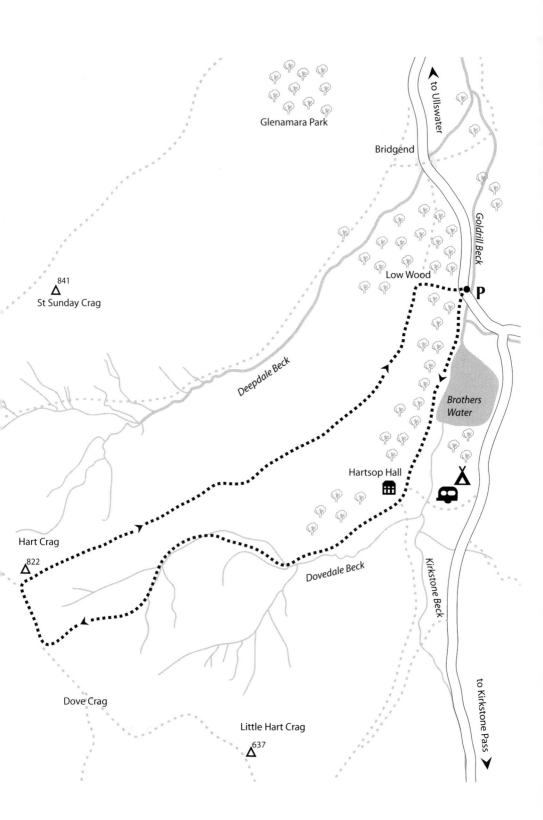

Glenamara Park

Bridgend

to Ullswater

Goldrill Beck

Low Wood

841
△
St Sunday Crag

Deepdale Beck

P

Brothers
Water

Hartsop Hall

Hart Crag

822
△

Dovedale Beck

Kirkstone Beck

to Kirkstone Pass

Dove Crag

Little Hart Crag

637
△

Brothers Water, Dovedale and the Hartsop valley

Grey wagtail

Start: Small car park off the A592
Grid Ref: NY404134
Distance: 6.1 miles (9.8km)
Grade: Easy to moderate
General: Toilets and refreshments in Patterdale (PT)

THIS IS A DELIGHTFUL circular walk in stunning scenery with all-year-round bird interest. The attractiveness was well known to Dorothy Wordsworth, who left William sitting on Cow Bridge and walked beside the lake on 16 April 1802. She was delighted with 'the boughs of the bare old trees, the simplicity of the mountains, and the exquisite beauty of the path … the gentle flowing of the stream, the glittering, lively lake'.

Formerly Broad Water, the name is said to have changed in the nineteenth century after two brothers drowned in it. This shallow lake is fringed with reed beds on the south side and in summer has a delightful blooms of water lilies. There is a wide range of habitats in quite a small area with stream, open water, mature broad-leaved woodland, open hillside with scattered trees, farmland and fell. There is an excellent National Trust map showing all the footpaths by the entrance gate.

From the small car park off the A592 take the wide woodland track which runs parallel with the stream and then up the valley past Brothers Water towards the sixteenth-century Hartsop Hall Farm.

❶ The stream with two bridges right next to the car park is a regular
haunt of both dipper and grey wagtail; at times both species have
nested in crevices on one or other of the bridges. When feeding young
there is a regular shuttle of visits just a few feet in front of you, for the
birds are not shy of man. Dippers, with their bobbing and curtseying
and half-cocked tail, are wonderful to watch. From the bridge if you
are lucky you can watch them dive and swim underwater with powerful
wing strokes, the clear water allowing wonderful views. Continue to
watch the stream and its several tributaries for more sightings of these
delightful birds, along with common sandpiper in spring and summer.

The star birds of the mature oak woodland of Low Wood are
pied flycatcher and redstart. With patience great views of these two
attractive summer visitors can be had, often singing or perching on
dead branches below the canopy. A wide range of other woodland
species including nuthatch, treecreeper and green and great spotted
woodpeckers also occur. Wood warblers used to be regular but have
become much rarer in recent years. In winter mixed tit flocks roam
the woods, with goldcrest, nuthatch, treecreeper and woodpeckers as
frequent camp followers.

In spring, on a warm morning or evening, the volume of song gives
a clue to the abundance of each species. Delightful though song may
be to our ears, however, we should always remember that the dual
purpose of song is to stake out and defend a territory and attract
a mate. Although there is variation between species, song output,
especially of resident species, varies through the season. There is an
early peak as territory is established, then a decline immediately after
pairing, followed by an increase during incubation, especially in those
species such as blackbird where the male does not incubate. But as
soon as the young are hatched there is a quick decline as both sexes
collect food for the young. If, however, eggs or young are predated,
song again increases and the cycle is repeated.

Red squirrels are regular here and a concerted campaign is being
waged to keep out the marauding, non-indigenous grey squirrel. Recent
estimates suggest that there are now about 2.5 million greys in England
and Wales, but there are only about 15,000 reds left in England. Let's
hope that the campaign is successful, for red squirrels are one of the
most attractive and well loved of our native mammals.

Brothers Water has breeding and wintering goosander, little grebe,
greylag and Canada geese, and occasionally great-crested grebe. The
best areas are usually near the inflow stream or the stony spit close to
the reed beds. Goosander and other wildfowl often haul out onto this
bare spit. The inflow and outlet streams are also popular with dipper,

grey wagtail and common sandpiper. The fringing reed beds are some distance from the path but support sedge warblers and reed buntings.

The woodland gradually thins out until only scattered trees are left. This is ideal habitat for tree pipits, conspicuous when they sing from tree tops and perform their aerial song flight. Redstarts and spotted flycatchers often favour the woodland edge. Stonechat and wheatear can be found among the scattered trees and bracken, while kestrels hover over the open areas and sparrowhawks use any available cover to mount an ambush. The iconic call of the cuckoo used to dominate this part of the valley, but they have declined recently and only small numbers now remain. Many other woodland birds occur in this habitat and the more open aspects makes spotting easier. The selective planting near Harsop Hall by the National Trust will in time extend and improve this habitat.

🚶 **The path divides just past Hartsop Hall Farm. Follow the path up Dovedale ignoring the first left-hand path By taking the next right-hand track it is possible to take a short cut up the very steep hillside, through a gate and make a return to the car park by turning right onto the well-worn path, then right again and back to the car park. The left-hand track crosses a footbridge and heads into Dovedale up the hill, taking two sharp right-hand turns past Dove and Hart Crags, and then follows the well-worn track back towards Patterdale. A right-hand turn down through Low Wood leads back to the car park.**

ⓘ Taking the longer more strenuous walk considerably increases the chances of sighting some of the scarcer open fell birds. Peregrines hunt the area from nearby crags and spend quite a lot of time perched silently on a rocky outcrop. When the smaller male returns he is greeted by a constant scolding call from the female and both will take to the air together revealing the marked size difference between the sexes. Merlins also visit from their heather-dominated breeding areas, often flying low over the ground in pursuit of a meadow pipit or other small bird. The blue-grey upperparts of the smaller male are striking as it dashes across the valley to be joined by the larger, brown female. Red grouse are rare but can be found among the larger heather patches. Ring ouzels occupy the rock-strewn hillsides, often preferring a small valley or ghyll. Meadow pipits are almost everywhere, along with smaller numbers of skylarks. Buzzards occur throughout the walk but are at their best rising on a thermal above the crags. Note their broad wings compared to the much slimmer, pointed wings of the falcons as exemplified by the kestrel that often hovers over the open hillside. On the return path there are many isolated trees and this gives a further opportunity to watch out for tree pipits, or even a green woodpecker straying out from Low Wood.

High Street, Riggindale and the Haweswater valley

Dotterel

Search for the golden eagle

Start: Small car park at the head of the Haweswater valley
Grid Ref: NY468107
Distance: Walk A 4.1 miles (6.6 km)
Walk B 7.1 miles (11.5 km)
Grade: Moderate for walk A, strenuous for walk B
General: Refreshment and toilet facilities can be found in
Shap village

W<small>E OFFER A CHOICE</small> of two walks here. The long walk (B) takes in some of the most spectacular country in Lakeland, with superb views of both the Kentmere and Haweswater valleys. It allows one to get a feel of the higher Lakeland fells and its admittedly scarce, but rather special, bird life. It should only be attempted by those fully equipped for fell walking as the paths are rough and at times difficult to follow without a map, and a GPS or compass. Walk A returns by the same route and gives a snapshot of the bird life of the lakeshore, woodland and lower fell.

Walk A: Riggindale

This short walk follows the well-used track down towards the lake over a footbridge across Mardale Beck and round the edge of the lake, eventually passing through the conifers of the Rigg then follows the path up the Riggindale valley. Return via the same route to the car park.

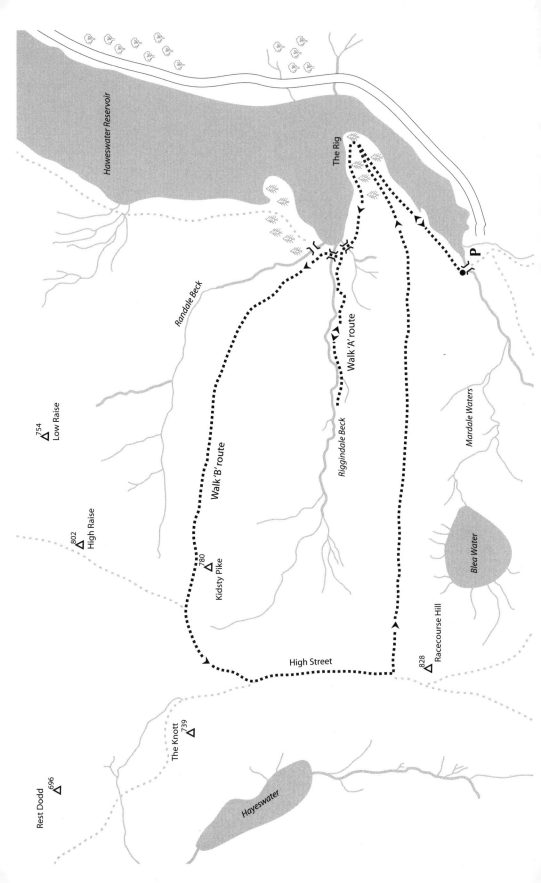

Haweswater Reservoir

The Rig

Randale Beck

Low Raise △⁷⁵⁴

High Raise △⁸⁰²

Walk 'B' route

Kidsty Pike △⁷⁸⁰

Rigindale Beck

Walk 'A' route

Mardale Waters

Blea Water

Racecourse Hill △⁸²⁸

High Street

Rest Dodd △⁶⁹⁶

The Knott △⁷³⁹

Hayeswater

P

❶ Dipper, grey wagtail and common sandpiper can be found on Mardale Beck, and also at times along the lakeshore. Water birds on or around the reservoir include goosander, great crested grebe, and red-breasted merganser. They are joined in winter by goldeneye and occasionally other diving ducks. A scan of the hillside will usually reveal wheatear and, if you are lucky, ring ouzel, as both tend to prefer rocky outcrops. Meadow pipits are common and cuckoos can be heard anywhere on the walk. Skylarks also prefer the open hillside, their song adding enrichment to any walk. The conifers of the Rigg harbour goldcrest and coal tit as regular breeding species but siskin and crossbill have occurred. From the shoreline of the Rigg, Wood Howe island can be seen. This was the site of a tree-nesting cormorant colony that reached 50 pairs in 1998, but because of concern over the impact this increasing population was having on the schelly, one of the lake's rare species of fish, control measures have been introduced in recent years and the cormorants may no longer nest. Other nesting birds on this island include both lesser black-backed and herring gulls, and greylag and Canada geese also breed here and elsewhere around the lake.

The scattered birches at the start of the Riggindale track hold redstarts, spotted flycatcher and at times redpolls. Scan the crags for ring ouzels; never an easy bird to find, patience will often be rewarded with good views of this evocative species flying along the crags, or best of all collecting food on the lower slopes. While scanning you will usually find small groups of red deer, part of the indigenous Martindale herd and very much at home on the steep hillsides of Kidsty Pike. But of course the bird everyone wants to see is England's only resident golden eagle. A pair nested in this valley for 32 years from 1969 on, rearing 16 young during this period. At the time of writing, sadly only a single male is resident in the area. The nest, which used to be almost as large as a double bed, can still be seen on one of the crags. Buzzards also occur of course, at times looking quite large as they take to the air, momentarily making the pulse race in the hope that here at last is the eagle. But in flight the golden eagle dwarfs the buzzard, being almost twice as large in wing span with large broad wings with 'fingered' tips and a powerful bill. The power of the bird shows in its flight, with typically a few wing beats followed by a long glide as it heads toward its perch on a rock or tree. Eagles spend many hours perched so a scan of suitable perching sites is well worthwhile.

On the walk back reflect on the changes that the flooding of the valley in 1935 to create a reservoir had on the former farming communities of Mardale Green and Measand. The buildings are now demolished and submerged but with low waters in summer the roads and walls – and at times the village bridge – become visible.

Walk B: Kidsty Pike/High Street

(X) **This long walk takes the track as described under the Riggindale walk but leaves it at the Rigg and follows the path across Riggindale Beck. Thereafter follow the obvious track over Kidsty Pike along the ridge to High Street.**

(i) With increasing altitude you leave behind the meadow pipits, skylarks and wheatears and begin to realise how few birds occur on the rather barren rock-strewn upper fells and on the highest Lakeland mountain tops. However, attention turns to birds in flight, which with increasing altitude often means you are looking down on them as they quarter the valley below. Ravens are one of the commonest, usually in pairs or later in the season family groups, but by late summer larger groups can be seen, especially if they have chosen to roost close by. The wonderful raucous 'cronk cronk' is usually the first warning that birds are approaching. They often mix, though not always amicably, with carrion crows when the larger size, wedge-shaped tail and powerful bill of the raven makes separation easy. The raven's flight is also much more powerful, with measured, driving wing beats. Ravens are one of the earliest nesters, often starting incubation during February when snow may still lying on the fells. Most nest on crags but with an increasing population, quarries and trees are now widely used.

Raven and carrion crows often tussle with peregrines, and such affrays can often last several minutes. However, peregrines are at their most impressive when hunting, best of all when they use the well-known stoop as with closed wings they hurtle down at great speed on their chosen prey, which on impact they knock with their feet. Pigeons, both wild and domestic, seem to be their favourite prey in this area.

Merlins occur occasionally but buzzards are common and they have contrasting hunting techniques. The smaller merlin preys mainly on small birds, especially meadow pipits. These are captured in flight after a vigorous close pursuit dashing low over the ground. By contrast buzzards adapt a 'wait-and-see' strategy, perching on rocks or trees as a look out before dropping onto some unsuspecting prey. At times they will also hover on their broad wings, watching for prey, followed by a quick swoop to catch its victim. Rabbits are their favourite prey but many smaller items are also taken, including many frogs in spring.

From High Street take the steep path along Long Stile and Rigindale Crag and down the steep slope to rejoin the path alongside the reservoir and back to the car park.

Again birds of prey are well-worth watching for. Peregrines regularly hunt or pass over from their valley breeding sites and kestrels hover over the lower slopes. But the highlight of any trip is a close view of a golden eagle gliding along the crags below you with large broad 'barn door' wings with fingered tips, leaving an indelible impression.

High Street at times also harbours two rather special birds: dotterel and snow bunting. Dotterel usually occur in small groups, for which the collective noun is 'trip', usually between late April and mid May when they pause on their migration from the wintering areas in Africa to the breeding grounds in Scotland. The habitat on High Street is very similar to that on the breeding grounds in the Cairngorms. They have a reputation for being very approachable.

Snow buntings occur in winter. These hardy birds breed widely across the arctic and a few pairs also on the tops of Scotland's highest mountains. They winter both on the high hills and along the coast, usually in small groups. Much of the plumage is white as their name suggests, and the white panels in the wing show well as they take to flight.

Swifts regularly occur over High Street, especially at migration times (late April to mid May and late July to August). They often skim the top of the ridge giving great views of this most aerial of birds. Numbers can also occur at any other times during their relatively short stay in Lakeland. Usually such occurrences can be linked to the weather, a thunderstorm for example, which displaces numbers from their usual feeding areas.

As you descend note how the breeding birds change both in numbers and species. There are few if any on the high tops, then gradually wheatears, meadow pipits and skylarks start to appear and increase in numbers. Once trees or scrub appear, especially in the small side valleys of Rigindale, willow warblers, tree pipits and redstarts should be looked for. If there is sufficient cover blackbirds, robin and chaffinches are added. Reaching the water, mallard, goosander and common sandpiper occur, while the crossing of Mardale Beck adds the possibility of grey wagtail and dipper.

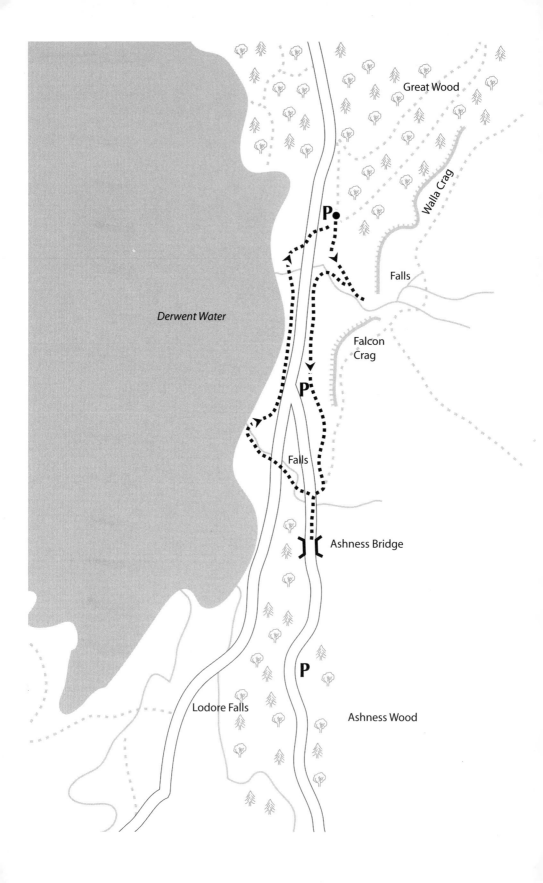

Great Wood

Walla Crag

Falls

P

Derwent Water

Falcon
Crag

P

Falls

Ashness Bridge

P

Lodore Falls

Ashness Wood

Great Wood to Ashness Bridge, Borrowdale valley

Pied flycatcher

Start: National Trust Great Wood car park
Grid Ref: NY272213
Distance: 2.8 miles (4.5 km)
Grade: Moderate
General: Toilets and all facilities in Keswick (PT)

THIS DRAMATIC AND ATTRACTIVE valley has wonderful views of Cat Bells to the west and Skiddaw to the north. Borrowdale is the most wooded of the Lakeland valleys and has many walking possibilities, ranging from the shores of Derwentwater, through the mainly steeply sloping mature woodland and out onto the open fell. The walk described here is on the accessible east shore of Derwentwater but many other walks are possible, including on the west shore which can be accessed by launch. The birds are very similar throughout the valley depending very much, of course, on habitat. This walk takes in the major habitats of the valley and so can also be used as a guide to most other walks.

⍲ **The walk starts in the National Trust car park at Great Wood. Take the path from the car park leading through the wood and up the hill. For this first section a short detour up the hill with a return to the bridge across the stream is recommended.**

❶ Several species can be seen and at times heard anywhere on the walk and these include buzzard, raven and peregrine, all of which breed close by and can often be seen in flight over the woods cliffs or open hillside.

The conifers around the car park have breeding goldcrest and coal tit. Although not exclusively restricted to conifers they are very typical and common birds of this habitat throughout the year. Siskin and occasionally crossbill have also been recorded.

Borrowdale has the largest block of sessile oak wood in northern Britain and because of this is an area of special conservation. From the start of the walk there are areas of mature, mainly oak woodlands, the breeding habitat of pied flycatcher, redstart and wood warbler. This latter species has recently declined in many areas but the extensive mature woodlands of Borrowdale are still one of the species strongholds and remain one of the easiest places to get to grips with this impressive little bird. It is the largest of the *phylloscupus* warblers and betrays its presence in spring by its most distinctive and remarkable dual song. The first part is a wonderful accelerating trill or shiver song followed by a rapidly repeated 'pew pew' note. The latter is often given on the wing but the shiver song is always delivered while perched. The song is regularly repeated as the bird moves from tree to tree, usually high in the canopy but with patience good views can be obtained. The steep slope of the wood helps to give better, almost eye level, views of the singing bird. It feeds almost exclusively within the canopy, either by catching any passing insect or by hovering with rapidly whirring wings as it neatly pecks an insect from the underside of a leaf. Wood warblers are ground nesters and need only minimal cover to hide their domed nest.

Other birds of the mature woodland include nuthatch, green and great spotted woodpeckers and treecreeper. Keeping to the path you would be very lucky to flush a woodcock. This an enigma of a bird, a woodland wader which spends the day on the woodland floor; heavily camouflaged it is almost impossible to spot. But at dusk and dawn this all changes as the male undertakes his amazing display, or territorial flight, called 'roding'. It gives a very distinctive grunting sound ending in an explosive note as it patrols just above the tree tops.

Within the woodlands are patches of thicker cover with a rich understory of hazel and at times bramble. These occur where large trees have fallen or been cut down and are an interesting contrast to the mature woodland close by. They provide suitable nesting sites for blackcap and garden warbler, summer visitors with remarkably similar songs. With experience they can be separated, as a general rule the blackcap gives shorter sweeter phrases, while the garden warbler gives much longer phrases, almost as though it will run out of breath.

In winter the woods often appear deserted – that is until a mixed flock of tits appears, then the woods are alive with birds for a few minutes. Blue and great tits usually make up the bulk of the flock but watch out for nuthatch and treecreeper, along with the occasional great spotted woodpecker and, if you are very lucky, a willow tit. If long-tailed tits are present they usually set a quicker pace and the flock moves quickly away.

🚶 **After returning from the detour cross over the stream by the bridge and out onto the open hillside. Continue along this well-worn path and at the first fork take the left-hand path signposted Ashness Bridge and continue until the road is reached.**

ⓘ Before moving out into the open area it is worth checking the woodland edge. Redstarts often sing at the edge and it is the favoured habitat of spotted flycatchers.

The open vista vastly improves the chances of seeing birds of prey – buzzard, sparrowhawk, peregrine and kestrel are regular, along with the occasional merlin. Ravens are also everywhere, their presence betrayed by the deep resonant croak. Tree pipits are a typical bird of this open habitat, singing from the tops of isolated trees before launching themselves into the air in a spectacular song flight, then parachuting down to the same or a different tree to repeat the performance. Other regular birds of this habitat include willow warbler, whitethroat and stonechat. Yellowhammers used to be common on these open habitats but numbers have declined and only a few now remain. The male is one of our most colourful and attractive birds and it is easy to trace as it delivers its well-known ditty of 'a little bit of bread and no cheese'. After the fork the scrub and gorse become quite thick, providing sufficient cover for bullfinch, long-tailed tit, blackcap and garden warbler and occasionally redpoll.

🚶 **On reaching the road go down the hill towards the lake. (To view the classic viewpoint of Derwentwater from Ashness Bridge it is necessary to take a slight deviation up the hill.)**

ⓘ The first section is close to the fast-flowing stream where there is always the chance of a dipper or grey wagtail. The road then passes through mixed woodland, giving a further chance to see some of the species already described for this habitat. In winter there is usually a marked movement of tits and finches towards the houses and the YHA hostel, no doubt attracted by well-stocked bird feeders, which demonstrates the importance of such feeding in winter. With them are usually nuthatch and great spotted woodpecker. There is a giant redwood, or wellingtonia, tree close to the road. The very soft and deep bark of this introduced tree provides ideal roosting hollows for treecreepers – evidence of their use is provided by the pile of droppings at the bottom of each hollow.

🚶 **On reaching the main lakeside road turn right and as soon as possible cross to the lakeside path and then proceed back to the car park.**

ⓘ The southern bays of Derwentwater are best for both breeding and wintering birds. Breeding birds include red breasted merganser, goosander, greylag and Canada geese. In winter flocks of diving ducks are regular, with numbers of pochard, goldeneye, tufted duck, the occasional grebes and more rarely divers. They regularly form a flock which frequently changes its position on the water. When feeding they are often close to the vegetated southern shore but when resting (or loafing as it is called) they usually seek the most sheltered side. Surface-feeding ducks also occur more erratically but numbers of teal and mallard often sit off the southern shore.

The Buttermere circuit

Redstart

Start and finish: Fish Hotel, Buttermere village
Grid Ref: NY175170
Distance: 5 miles (8.1 km)
Time: Four hours
Grade: Easy
General: Refreshment, toilet and parking facilities at
Buttermere village (PT)

THE FOCUS OF THIS walk is the lovely Buttermere Lake, owned by the National Trust, as indeed is almost a quarter of the land within the Lake District National Park. The Buttermere valley is flanked by some of the wildest and highest peaks in Lakeland. Down below, and in stark contrast to the mountaintops, Buttermere and nearby Crummock Water nestle in a beautiful green glacial valley. Overall the scenery is quite superb, especially looking towards the Newlands valley and the dramatic Honister Pass.

The described Buttermere circuit offers a comfortable circular walk along easy paths. Quite naturally the walk is very popular with walkers and during high summer weekends there may well be more people than birds. Thus it is recommended that to enjoy the walk at its bird-watching best it should be done in late April or early May, ideally on weekdays and as early in the day as possible.

From the village centre go left of the Fish Hotel and walk along a bridleway to the northern shore of Buttermere Lake. Commence a straightforward and waymarked anticlockwise walk around the lake to Gatescarth Farm. At Gatesgarth Farm turn left and walk along the road towards Buttermere village for a short distance to

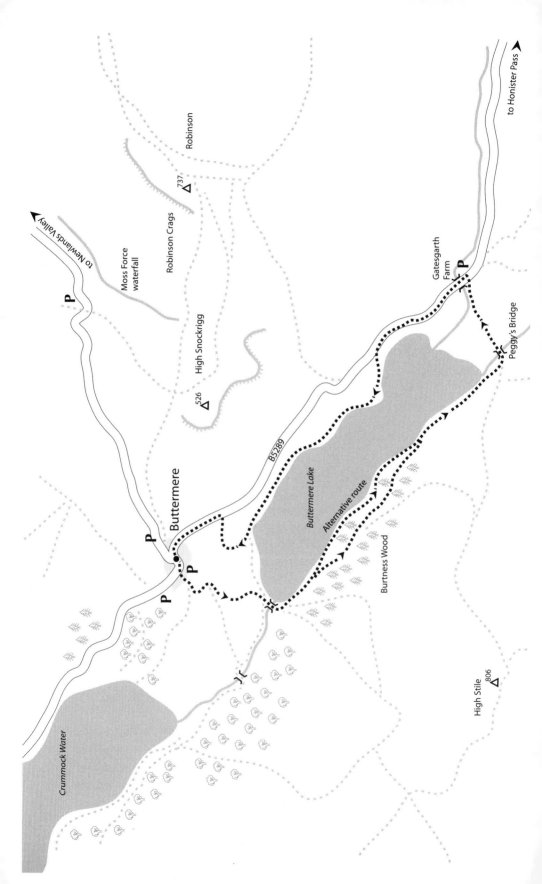

to Newlands Valley

P

Moss Force waterfall

Robinson Crags

Robinson

737

High Snockrigg

526

to Honister Pass

Gatesgarth Farm

P

Peggy's Bridge

B5289

Buttermere

P
P
P

Buttermere Lake

Alternative route

Burtness Wood

Crummock Water

High Stile

806

where the footpath diverges left towards the lake edge. Follow the permissive foopath between rocky outcrops and the edge of the lake, passing through an unusual pedestrian tunnel hewn in rock. Proceed along the path to eventually fork right in order to rejoin the road near Buttermere village and return to the starting point.

❶ Around the village of Buttermere the majority of garden birds are typically woodland-edge species. Song thrush, blackbird, dunnock, chaffinch, greenfinch, goldfinch, nuthatch, great spotted woodpecker and an assortment of titmice are regular on garden bird tables and well-stocked feeding stations, an abundance of birds that attracts the superbly adapted sparrowhawk. Not surprisingly, they exploit this availability of prey and consequently may be seen making a quick dash from the neighbouring woods to snatch a tasty morsel for the plucking post, where the raptor dismembers its catch.

As well as the sparrowhawk, a close relative may be seen in the form of the rare and impressive goshawk, a species of both deciduous and conifer woodlands and wild open spaces. Goshawks can sometimes occur over vast peripheral areas of the Lake District and a chance encounter with this rare and enigmatic species flying over the woodlands and open areas surrounding the lake is within the realms of possibility. Identification skills are put to the test here, though, and care should be taken in distinguishing goshawk from similar species, including the resident sparrowhawk and the more numerous buzzards.

The first section of the walk incorporates pastoral fields divided by sturdy hedgerows, where certain of the aforementioned species may well be observed, together with migrating swallows hawking for insects and the flocks of jackdaws that are such a feature of Lakeland. At the head of the lake the confluence with Buttermere Dubs is a good place to see the semi-aquatic dipper flying or alighting on stones along the river. Common sandpiper, pied and grey wagtail are distinct possibilities here and indeed anywhere around the edge of lake.

Ahead are the hanging oak and conifer woodlands that constitute Burtness Wood. The mixed woodland provides a good habitat for a variety of birds and mammals, including the native red squirrel. Fortunately at the time of writing, the local population at Burtness Wood has not been infiltrated by the greys.

On entering the wood it is recommended that the upper loop path be taken in preference to the lakeside path, as the former is quieter and affords better opportunities for birding. The best way to observe woodland birds is to sit quietly and comfortably and let them come to you. Ideally this should be done in spring before oak buds have fully burst and the foliage has transformed the canopy into a deeper shade of green and yellow. From your elevated position listen and watch for movement in the trees. Check for flocks of typical woodland birds – 'bird parties' – passing through the canopy which may consist of great spotted woodpecker, chaffinch, bullfinch, treecreeper, nuthatch, goldcrest, coal and long-tailed tits.

The characteristic chirpings of crossbills usually indicate the presence of very nice brick-red males, yellow-green females and streaked brown immature birds that are often conspicuously perched in the tops of larch and pine while busily devouring cones. A good view reveals that the upper and lower mandibles are indeed crossed and that the incredibly powerful bill is the perfect tool for the job.

In exultation of the forthcoming breeding season a mistle thrush proudly delivers its wild and somewhat fluty mournful song from the tops of the tallest trees in order to establish its territory and attract a mate. In spring the woods are alive with the sounds of contrasting bird song and when compared with the mistle thrush the melodic tones of the blackbird are delightfully mellow. Unlike humans, birds do not sing because they are happy. The song serves two main functions, both part of the breeding cycle. Firstly, song is important in establishing a bird's territory; it advertises that a territory is occupied and warns trespassers away. Secondly, during the early part of the breeding season the male's song gives notice to a potential female that he has established a territory and is ready to mate.

A variety of warblers sing beautifully to establish their territories, and typically chiffchaff, willow warbler and blackcap make for a worthy ornithological chorus. Willow warblers, with their liquid cadence, descend the scales in their own special way, while the similar plumage of the chiffchaff is belied by the repetitive chiff-chaff call that give it its name. The loud vibrating rattle produced by rapidly repeated blows of its strong bill upon a tree or branch represents the territorial claim of the great spotted woodpecker, occasionally interspersed by its 'kik kik' alarm call. In this avian chorus the woodpecker adds his own touch of percussion, while overhead the raven makes up the brass section with its instantly recognisable deep 'pruck pruck' trumpeting calls.

However, the real maestro of northern woodlands is the wood warbler. Listen and watch for the yellow tints of this 'leaf warbler,' as it busily flits about in the fresh green foliage. Another fine contender for a soloist part in this lovely cacophony is the tree pipit. This species prefers more open spaces in woodlands where it can descend from the highest tree in a spectacular parachuting aerial display, while simultaneously performing its superb trilling aerial song. The handsome male redstart, siskin and pied flycatcher should also be looked for in the extensive conifer and deciduous woodland habitat, though their vocal prowess hardly qualifies them as lead vocalists. In fact the benign reel of the redstart and rasping song of the pied flycatcher are never more than a mere prelude! Together with tree pipit this particular trio do not rely heavily on woodland and may be seen in Burtness Wood and in suitable areas on either side of the lake.

Emerging from extensive woodlands the footpath passes below bracken-covered slopes and then bisects farmland, with views of the famous scattering of Scots pine that characterise the shore of the south-east end of the lake. The open vistas here are likely to produce buzzard, kestrel and raven flying alongside the cliffs, while at a lower altitude the slopes are the haunts of both the wheatear and meadow pipit. Resident breeding peregrine falcons are likely to turn up anywhere, often when least expected. Listen out for the harsh yak-yak-yak call resounding from lofty crags, always a give away for the presence of this splendid falcon.

Following the return route from Gatesgarth Farm, wheatears may be seen bobbing about on rock-strewn hills and on walls close to the road. The permissive footpath traverses a different sort of habitat that is less densely wooded. Family parties of long-tailed tits can often be seen and there may be further opportunities to observe tree pipit and redstart. Willow warblers are invariably present and garden warbler and blackcap are both possible, together with a supporting cast of the more usual suspects such as wood pigeon, chaffinch, blackbird and the ubiquitous wren.

Good views of the lake from an elevated position usually reveal a few mallards and black-headed gulls on the surface, a situation not untypical for the deeper glacial lakes, and certainly nothing to get excited about. Introduced greylag geese have become naturalised in most of the Lake District. Nevertheless gaggles of greylag and/or Canada geese are unlikely to command much attention from serious aficionados unless the flock harbours a vagrant visitor. Instead save your enthusiasm for sightings of red-breasted mergansers and even visiting ospreys, rather than the resident feral greylags!

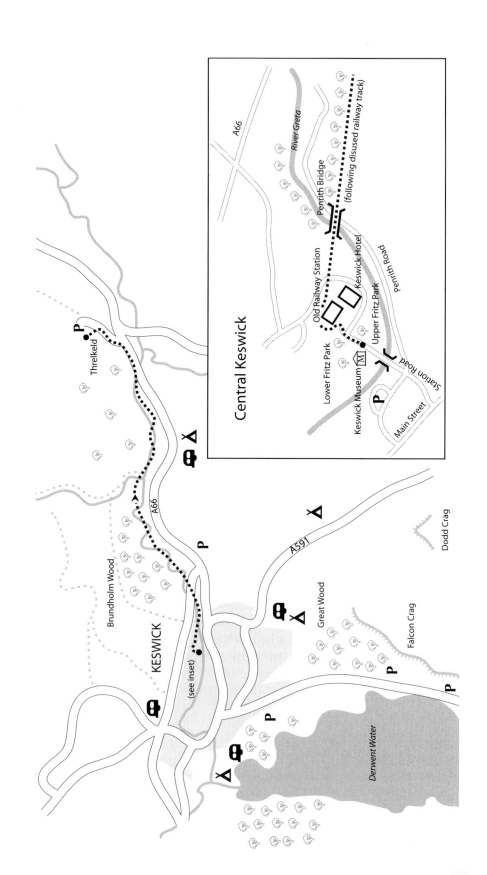

Central Keswick

River Greta

A66

Penrith Bridge

(following disused railway track)

Old Railway Station

Keswick Hotel

Penrith Road

Upper Fritz Park

Lower Fritz Park

Keswick Museum

Station Road

P

Main Street

Threlkeld

P

Brundholm Wood

A66

P

KESWICK

(see inset)

P

Great Wood

A591

Dodd Crag

Falcon Crag

P

P

Derwent Water

From Keswick to Threlkeld

Oystercatcher

'Walking the line' – with a single ticket

Start: Keswick Museum, Station Road
Grid Ref: NY268237
Distance: 4 miles (6.4 km)
Time: Three hours
Grade: Easy
General: Toilet, refreshment and parking facilities at Keswick and Threlkeld (PT)

THIS POPULAR RAILWAY WALK follows the course of the most idyllic stretch of a former branch line. The celebrated poet John Ruskin complained of the new railways unloading trippers like sacks of coal at Windermere. Likewise William Wordsworth also expressed doubts about railways being compatible with the rural scene. It is also true, however, that for many years the local branch lines alleviated vehicular pressure on Lakeland's narrow roads. The old Keswick branch line has now gone full circle since those early days by being integrated into the landscape of the Greta gorge to the east of Keswick. Today there is still an abundance of wildlife along several disused branch lines that have been transformed into footpaths and linear nature reserves throughout Cumbria. Perhaps the two venerable poets would ultimately have approved after all!

The surviving four miles of the old track bed and infrastructure from Keswick through the Greta gorge to Threlkeld were purchased by the Lake District National Park Authority in 1983 and today make up one of the most spectacular railway walks in the country. The walk commences at the former Keswick railway station and crosses eight impressive bowstring bridges spanning the River Greta, which have been colonised by nesting jackdaws. At one stage a boardwalk diverts the walker around a blocked-off tunnel and the track later passes through a short tunnel. Throughout the walk the views over the River Greta are awe-inspiring and so is the wildlife.

Ⓐ **To reach the starting point walk along Station Road past Fitz Park and museum and cross over the River Greta. At Keswick Leisure Centre turn left and walk around the rear of the complex to arrive at the old railway station. Commence the four-mile railway walk along the disused railway to Threlkeld. After the eighth viaduct spanning the picturesque and ornithologically rich River Greta the walk leaves the old track bed and continues for quarter of a mile to the village. At Threlkeld adequate refreshments are available at either of the two village pubs, where you can conclude a superb bird watching walk before catching the hourly bus back to Keswick or Penrith.**

ⓘ En route to the site of the old Keswick railway station (the main station building remains and is today partly used as bedroom accommodation for the hotel) spend a bit of time bird watching in the delightful Fitz Park on the banks of the River Greta. You might wish to consider a visit to Keswick's free museum and art gallery on Station Road, which first opened on the 11 April, 1898, to replace the museum housed in the old moot hall. The museum has an interesting collection of British stuffed birds, mammals and local history exhibits including material from the closed railway. On the walk we focus on some of the animals and birds which are housed in the museum collection and look forward to seeing pristine live specimens rather than faded museum exhibits in glass cases.

   The walk closely follows the fast-flowing River Greta as it tumbles over rocks and meanders through deciduous oak woods, and it is certainly to be recommended for its considerable charm, historical interest and excellent bird watching potential. There is a good chance of seeing oystercatcher, common sandpiper, heron, dipper, pied and grey wagtail, goldeneye, red-breasted merganser and goosander. The latter two species are described as sawbills because their long, narrow, serrated bills are well suited to catching and holding slippery prey. The goosander nests in holes in trees and during May look out for family parties with up to eight or twelve ducklings. While they are an appealing sight, both sawbills are the only ducks that habitually fish for a living and they therefore compete with, and are certainly not popular with, the local fishermen. By contrast, that other renowned angler, the kingfisher, makes for convivial company during long periods of solitude and has even been known to perch on fishing rods. It may be possible to observe this beautiful creature, but on this particular walk there is certainly no guarantee.

As you walk along the railway track long-tailed tits can often be seen in family groups. Look out for bird parties that might include mixed flocks of blue, great, coal and long-tailed tit, wren, goldcrest, treecreeper and nuthatch. Of the common resident birds the familiar chaffinch is probably the most numerous. Greenfinch, goldfinch, lesser redpoll and siskin represent other members of the finch family. Great spotted woodpecker and the colourful jay are likely to turn up when least expected. Willow warbler, spotted and pied flycatcher and redstart are typical summer visitors that are to be found in the dominant oak woods that line the river throughout the walk. What a fantastic bird the redstart is, so exquisite with its slate-grey back and wings, brick-red breast contrasting with a black throat and a white forehead. The rich chestnut quivering tail is ever in motion and catches the eye as it flits from branch to branch. The contrasting female of the species is less bright and has a soft brown plumage but with the same distinctive red tail.

Beautiful as the redstart is, the wood warbler also takes some beating. If you are lucky you may hear the accelerating trill and flute-like crescendo of this rather special gem of a bird as it characteristically flits through the fresh green foliage. By contrast, there is nothing very distinctive about the garden warbler's appearance. It is an olive-brown, medium-sized warbler that may be distinguished from the closely related blackcap by the absence of the black crown of the male blackcap. Keep your eyes and ears open for both species for the song is crucial in locating them. The garden warbler's song is a lovely continuous mellow warble, longer and more sustained than the blackcap, but nevertheless not easy to distinguish and likely to cause confusion.

Fishermen are often out in the peace and quiet of dawn and dusk on the riverbank, but seldom do they see an otter along this stretch of the River Greta, although they are undoubtedly present. Red squirrels are, at least for the time being, still fairly abundant and are likely to be observed at several points along the walk, especially where there are feeders. As you leave the old track bed and walk towards Threlkeld take note of the special red squirrel road sign warning drivers of the equivalent of pedestrian crossings for squirrels.

Whinlatter Forest Park

Buzzard

Start: Whinlatter Forest Visitor Centre
Grid Ref: NY209245
Grade: Easy to strenuous
General: Toilets, refreshments and shop (maps are available)
at the Visitor Centre (PT)

A VISIT TO THIS FOREST PARK can be rewarded by the sight of two typically coniferous specialists – siskin and crossbill. Both are relatively recent colonists of Lakeland, their spread a result of the widespread planting of conifer forests by the Forestry Commission

There is a wide variety of walks within the forest park that cater for all abilities. The walks are indicated by coloured waymarkers and an excellent map, available from the visitor centre.

Of the eight walks detailed on the forest map five are recommended for bird watching. The maps give an estimate of time that should be allowed for each walk. However, when bird watching progress is usually slower with frequent stops, so this should be taken into consideration when you start out. As a general rule of thumb allow at least half as much time again as given on the map.

Whinlatter was the first forest to be planted by the newly formed Forestry Commission in 1919 following the timber shortage after World War One. It is of course a working forest with areas being thinned or clear felled and replanted, so the habitat and the birds can change very quickly. However, there are several distinct habitats within the forest and because the walks are so well waymarked no detailed directional instructions are needed, so in these walks the bird species are described by habitat.

Walks starting at the visitor centre

(walker icon) **There are three trails starting and returning to the visitor centre that are recommended for bird watching: the red-marked Comb Forest Trail (1.75 miles, 2.8 km); the blue-marked Comb Gill Trail (1.75 miles, 2.8 km) both these being graded as moderate; and the green-marked Seat How Summit Trail (3.5 miles, 5.75 km) graded as strenuous.**

(i) Because of the dense, regimented structure of coniferous forest birds are hard to find, but there are several specialists that are well worth looking for. The edge of a conifer block where it changes to one of the other habitats is the best place to watch. Goldcrests, our smallest bird, are common. When feeding they delicately search the conifers, flitting gracefully from twig to twig. They call regularly, a very high pitched 'si si' note. But beware, those of advancing years may have difficulty in picking up this high-pitched call, and also its song which is a quick repetition of two notes. The nest is a wonderfully neat hammock suspended beneath a branch. The other common bird is the coal tit, and this hole-nesting species overcomes the almost complete lack of tree holes in a commercial forest by nesting in holes in the ground, or in the rotting bole of a tree.

Siskins are our smallest finch and for breeding are restricted to conifer woods. Tit-like in their acrobatic feeding behaviour, they are easily located by their distinctive call and song, the latter often given on the wing. Once found they can be quite approachable. In winter they move out of the conifers and can often be found with redpolls feeding on alder seed, and later in the winter they come in numbers to bird feeders. The iconic bird of conifers, however, is the crossbill. It takes its name, of course, from its most striking and distinctive feature, the crossed tips of the mandibles, an adaption that allows it to open the spruce, larch and pine cones with ease. The lovely red plumage of the male stands out against the green of the trees but the grey-green females and immature males are more difficult to spot. They feed silently in the tree tops, their movements parrot-like as they clamber along the branches, often walking sideways and reaching down to wrench off a cone. But as they take flight the very distinctive 'chip chip' call is given. Often the first signs that they are around is a litter of cones beneath the trees, or best of all a cone dropping from the branches. The scales of the cones are split, unlike those chopped by red squirrels which are stripped. Numbers breeding in the forest vary greatly from year to year. After large influxes reach Britain from northern Europe following a failure of pine cones, their principle food, the numbers staying to breed are high, but as such arrivals only occur every few years the population drops back until the next irruption.

Native red squirrel are very much at home in conifers and Whinlatter has a good population, so watch out for their dreys and the tell-tale stripped cones. Several feeding sites are in operation but it is best to ask at the visitor centre for directions. Roe deer are common and in some areas are so used to visitors that they remain calmly browsing as you pass.

Regenerated, cleared and replanted areas are scattered among the conifers and make an interesting contrast to the regimented pine forest. Especially good is a section on the blue walk where there is a plot of newly established broad-leaved trees. As you leave the mature conifer stands with little or no under growth or ground flora, the change is quite startling. Regenerating native trees such as birch, willow, ash and oak provide cover. Many areas have a thick growth of gorse, bramble and raspberry. The ground flora is dominated by grasses and in some areas heather. With the sun flooding in many insects, including common butterflies and dragonflies, flourish. Warblers find this to their liking too and willow warblers are common, while the dry reeling song of the grasshopper warbler also can be heard along with the quick short jerky verse of the whitethroat. With thick cover both blackcap and garden warbler can be found taxing your ability to separate their songs. Redpolls quickly move into the regenerating areas while spotted flycatchers prefer the woodland edge. In some areas good thickets of gorse have emerged which attract linnets and whitethroats and are a favourite nesting site for long-tailed tits.

With a wider horizon birds of prey are easier to see here. These include buzzard, sparrowhawk and kestrel, with peregrine and merlin always a possibility. An excellent way to end a walk is to visit the aptly named Siskins Café in the visitor centre. The well-stocked feeders are visited by siskins for much of the year, allowing excellent close views. One of the commonest birds visiting the feeders is coal tit. It is fascinating to watch their contrasting feeding behaviour. Some stop at the feeders for up to a minute, taking their fill, while others nip in quickly and fly off with a seed or nut which they will hide in some suitable hole or crevice, for this species regularly caches food. Studies have shown that they successfully retrieve the food weeks or even months after first hiding it.

❶ On the green walk up to Utlister Hill the track passes through a third type of habitat in the form of open heather moorland. Look out for meadow pipit and wheatear. Where there is heather, stonechat and red grouse may be found along with merlin and ring ouzel.

Walks from Noble Knott car park

(walker icon) **The white waymarked Noble Knott Heavy Sides Trail (1.5 miles, 2.5 km) and the black waymarked Noble Knot Masmill Beck Trail (1.25 miles, 2 km) are both graded as moderate. Both walks are recommended for bird watching and are very well waymarked so no directions are necessary.**

(info icon) These two circular walks give the visitor the opportunity to experience the marked contrast between native mature oak woodland and planted conifers. There are, however, only limited areas of pure oak forest, although planting is taking place to extend these native woodlands. Much of these two walks pass through areas of mixed woodland with patches of native, mainly oak, woodland mixed with a variety of planted conifers. Because of this mixed habitat a good range of species occurs and several species show a marked preference for a particular habitat.

However, the first noticeable difference is in the ground flora – almost totally absent under the dense, regimented spruce stands but dominated by bracken and grasses with a limited range of native flowers under the oak trees. With a few exceptions birds are more abundant and more visible within the oak stands. A variety of natural holes within the ancient oaks provides nest sites for blue and great tit, along with pied flycatcher, redstart and treecreeper. Great spotted and green woodpeckers make their own nesting holes, which are used in successive seasons by other hole-nesting species including starlings. The open areas around the oaks with the good ground cover provide ample nesting sites for willow warblers. Of the finches, chaffinch and redpoll prefer the native woodland and especially the cleared conifer areas which are regenerating, with a good variety of native tree species.

The commonest breeding birds in the conifers are coal tit and goldcrest, with siskin and crossbill always possible. One advantage of the mixed woodland is that it provides a great deal of edge to the conifers and this, combined with the sloping ground, means that good views are possible over varying distances. So if these birds are present the chances of seeing them are much better than in the pure dense conifer stands.

In winter once the leaves have dropped, and because of the good vistas in these areas, this is probably the best area within the park to see crossbills, particularly in years with a good cone crop. They can be surprisingly quiet and as they clamber parrot-like in the canopy they are not always easy to pick out, especially the grey-green birds. Within the regenerating areas there are numbers of berry-bearing trees and shrubs which attract numbers of wintering thrushes early in the winter. Because of the proximity to the large area of conifers, winter tit flocks have a high proportion of coal tits, while they usually attract goldcrests and treecreepers in smaller numbers.

Dodd Wood, Bassenthwaite

Great spotted woodpecker

A quest for pandion haliaetus

Start: Dodd Wood Visitor Centre, situated three miles north of Keswick just off the A591, and on the east side of Bassenthwaite Lake (PT)

Grid Ref: NY235282

Grade: Moderate climb especially at beginning of walk to the nest site

Distance: Approximately 2 miles (3.2 km)

Time: Allow four hours or spend the whole day at the two viewpoints

General: (See map on page 42.) There are two official viewpoints to view the ospreys and both are situated in Dodd Wood. Both are normally open between Easter and October, the lower viewpoint is open 10am – 5pm and the upper viewpoint 10.30am – 4.30pm. Car park, toilets and refreshments at Dodd Wood and Whinlatter visitor centres, where guide books for nature trails may be purchased.* (See also walk eight for details of Whinlatter.) Most of the eastern shoreline of Bassenthwaite is privately owned, with restricted footpath access and for paying visitors to Mirehouse House and gardens

K ESWICK IS THE NEAREST TOWN, and the 'osprey bus' operates from here during summer weekends, serving both centres. At Whinlatter a video link

---

* The following guide outlining the history of the Lakeland ospreys is available for sale at the centre: Ramshaw, D., *The Lake District Osprey Project*, P3 Publications, Carlisle (2002), cost £5.

relays live pictures from the nest direct to the centre for public viewing. The actual nest-viewing site is at Dodd Wood (check the opening times of the two forward observation viewpoints). Staff from the Osprey Project partnership will be on hand with telescopes, but in wet weather the telescopes may be removed. (Lake District Osprey Project website – www.ospreywatch.co.uk.)

(🚶) **Enjoy the following walk in anticipation of seeing live ospreys at the nest. From the car park follow the waymarked path up through woodland to the lower viewpoint. Be aware that the first part of the walk is steeply graded and it takes approximately fifteen minutes to reach the first viewpoint. This is the original viewpoint and although the nest site cannot be seen, good views are afforded of the northern end of the lake, where it may be possible to watch an osprey fishing. To continue, regain the path and ascend a moderate incline, taking approximately forty five minutes to reach the upper viewpoint.**

🛈 Dodd Wood supports a range of birds and other wildlife, and a feeding station at the lower viewpoint attracts jay, great spotted woodpecker, robin, coal, blue and great tits, and, with a bit of luck, red squirrel. However, on this particular walk the focus is on one bird, the spectacular osprey, *pandion haliaetus – pandion* after the mythical King of Athens, and *haliaetus* from the Greek *hals* and *aetus* for 'sea,' and 'eagle.' What a great name for a rather special bird that since 2001 has bred annually in woodlands around Bassenthwaite Lake that are managed by the Forestry Commission. Ospreys returned to breed at the famous Loch Garten site in the Highlands of Scotland in 1954–55 after being extinct as a British breeding species since the time of the last Scottish nest in 1916.

The Lakeland ospreys are an integral part of this wildlife success story that has since seen the osprey population expand to its present level of 180 pairs. It was not until 1999 that a nest was found at a secret site in Cumbria – not Bassenthwaite – that sadly failed to rear young. These birds returned in 2000 and this time successfully reared a single chick; a particularly significant event as it was the first successful nest in England since 1842. In anticipation of future breeding successes, the Lake District Osprey Project, a partnership of the Forestry Commission, Lake District National Park Authority and the RSPB, was formed in 2000 to work together to safeguard the ospreys.

The osprey's habitat is governed by the bird's total dependence on an abundant supply of medium-sized fish near the surface of clear unpolluted water. Bassenthwaite Lake clearly fulfils these criteria with a variety of over ten different species of fish, including the very rare vendace, a species of fish found in deep water and thus not normally available to the osprey. Typical prey species include perch, roach, trout, eels and small pike. The fishing osprey is spectacular to watch; fish are caught in the bird's talons after a shallow dive with wings half folded and feet projected at the last moment as the bird plunges into water that is no deeper than one metre. Once caught the fish is turned to face head first to reduce air resistance as the osprey flies to a favoured perch or to the nest site.

At Bassenthwaite a lack of suitable nest sites was identified as a major problem and therefore a nest platform was built in Wythop Woods close to the Whinlatter Pass, overlooking the lake. In 2001 all the hard work paid off and a pair of osprey nested on the platform for the first time and successfully reared one chick. Ospreys usually lay three eggs in an amazing nest that can be up to the size of a double bed! The eggs take about six weeks to hatch and the young stay in the nest for a further six to seven weeks. All the chicks are ringed, measured, weighed and photographed when they are five or six weeks old. This information is recorded to help identify the birds and to monitor their development.

The male does most of the fishing, providing food for the female and young. In late summer the female migrates south to Africa, leaving the male to teach the young how to fish. A few weeks later, in September, the male and young also head for the warmer climes of West Africa where they might be observed in the Gambia and Senegal. Normally it will not be until early April of the following year that the first osprey may be seen in the skies above Bassenthwaite, having undertaken a flight of approximately 3,000 miles. Males and females spend the winter apart but miraculously the same birds meet up at the nest in spring within days of each other, just one of the mysteries of migration.

During the inaugural 2001 season over 25,000 people, comprising keen birdwatchers, the local community and holidaymakers of all ages, visited the viewpoint in ten weeks. Under twenty four-hour supervision by the Osprey Project team the ospreys have nested every year since at Bassenthwaite. However, since 2008 the pair has selected a new nest site in Dodd Wood, which at approximately 500 yards away is much closer to the viewpoint than the original site. The hope is that the Bassenthwaite osprey population will continue to expand during the coming years; indeed nowadays they may be seen fishing a number of lakes, thus enriching Lakeland by adding the finishing touches to some of most spectacular scenery in Britain.

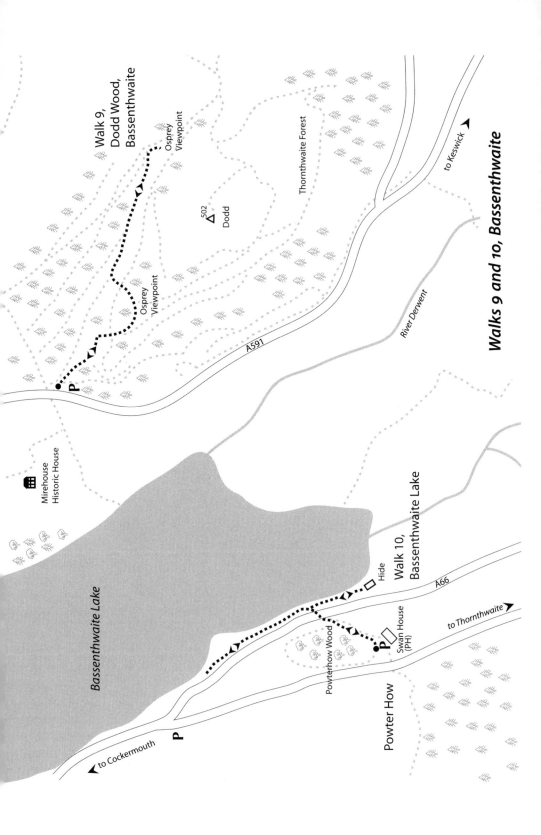

Walk 9, Dodd Wood, Bassenthwaite

Osprey Viewpoint

Osprey Viewpoint

502 Dodd

Thornthwaite Forest

A591

River Derwent

to Keswick

Mirehouse Historic House

Bassenthwaite Lake

to Cockermouth

Walk 10, Bassenthwaite Lake

Hide

Powterhow Wood

Swan House (PH)

A66

to Thornthwaite

Powter How

Walks 9 and 10, Bassenthwaite

Bassenthwaite Lake

Whooper swan

Ospreys and supporting cast

Start and finish: The car park at Swan House, Thornthwaite, situated two miles north of Braithwaite alongside an unclassified road paralleling the A66 (PT)

Grid Ref: NY235282

Distance: 3 miles (4.8 km)

Time: Four hours

Grade: Easy

General: There is a large car park situated outside Swan House, toilets and refreshments at Dodd Wood and Whinlatter visitor centres. The osprey viewpoint at Dodd Wood is accessed from Mirehouse visitor centre (see previous walk). The serenity of the lake and its important wildlife justifies restricted boating and the most important site for breeding and over-wintering birds at the southern end of the lake is a no-boating zone. To the north west of the bird hide good views may be had of the lake and the steep, mixed deciduous and conifer woods that comprise Wythop Woodlands

THE DESCRIBED WALK IS through Powerhow Wood to a bird watching hide at the south-western end of Bassenthwaite Lake. The hide provides excellent views of the lake and extensive reed.

🚶 **From the car park go through the gate and along the public footpath through Powerhow woodlands, to a subway below the A66, emerging close to the lakeshore. Turn right and take the**

footpath south through woodland to a bird hide. From the hide retrace your steps and continue to walk along the woodland path. There is an option to extend the walk by walking north towards Cockermouth along the footpath next to the A66. However, for the discerning walker the views of the lake and the dominant mountain of Skiddaw will probably be compromised by the constant roar of traffic and detract from the aesthetics. Walk as far as you want before retracing your steps to the starting point.

ⓘ Bassenthwaite Lake has the unique distinction of being the only one in the Lake District to officially be described as a lake. All the others use the word water or mere. Bassenthwaite Lake's other claim to fame is that it is a National Nature Reserve and Site of Special Scientific Interest, owned and managed by the Lake District National Park Authority. The mixed woodlands on both sides of the lake are mostly owned by the Forestry Commission, and support a diverse range of birds and other wildlife. As well as the famous nesting pair of ospreys, Bassenthwaite plays host to a supporting cast of over seventy breeding species of birds, thus ranking it as perhaps the finest bird watching locality within the National Park. In addition, the reserve plays host to a rich flora represented by the localised globe flower, betony and swathes of purple loosestrife, which in turn attract an interesting range of insects including dragonflies and butterflies, adding even more sparkle and interest.

The predominant mixture of beech and oak woodland around Powterhow supports good populations of siskin, lesser redpoll, pied flycatcher, wood warbler and redstart. At the time of writing the redstart is maintaining its numbers in Lakeland, but unfortunately the status of the wood warbler, tree pipit and spotted flycatcher, which used to be regular and well-distributed summer visitors to the area, has now changed and in many areas they no longer co-exist or have become scarce.

At the southern extremity of the lake, Braithwaite bog is important as a unique and rare fen habitat, embracing mire, redbud, alder, birch, shingle banks and islands. Access and viewing over this specialised habitat and flood plain is very restricted, allowing a diversity of wildlife to exploit the area fully. In spring the charismatic lapwing, crying out its alternative name of peewit, and the drumming of the snipe over their preferred habitats of unimproved grasslands and wet meadows, is a sight to behold. In complete contrast the tiny grasshopper warbler is a mainly shade-loving species that is likely to be found on Braithwaite bog. They are usually located at the top of a tuft of grass or in a small bush, with beak open wide while delivering their intriguing continuous reeling song.

The hide is situated on the edge of the lake at Powterhow and is ideal for scanning the open water and extensive reed beds. Breeding wildfowl, reed buntings, and sedge and reed warblers are seldom disturbed except by patrolling predators. Fishing is prohibited in the waters near the bird hide but regular sightings of kingfishers here would tend to imply that they have not read the rules! Grey wagtail, common sandpiper, redshank and oystercatcher are often conspicuous on the stony shores, taking advantage of fluctuating water levels for food and possible nest sites. Mammal sightings are possible here and there is a good chance of seeing up to three otters fishing and playing. Roe deer may also be spotted feeding at the edge of the lake and woodland fringe.

At times in winter there are likely to be over 1,000 surface-feeding and diving ducks of various species at the southern end of the lake devouring the submerged vegetation, seeds, small fish and invertebrates. These flocks are likely to embrace tufted duck, teal, goosander, goldeneye, pochard, mallard, wigeon and occasional unusual species such as smew, common scoter, scaup, long-tailed duck and red-throated diver. Flocks of mute and whooper swans are also regular in winter, together with coot, cormorant, great crested grebe, goosander, red-breasted merganser and greylag geese. At appropriate seasons the diversity of habitat around the lake attracts several species of raptors and any of the following are possibilities: buzzard, peregrine falcon, kestrel, merlin, kestrel, hen harrier, barn owl, sparrowhawk, and of course during spring and summer, the osprey. Watching ospreys fishing the lake is an amazing site which can be enjoyed from the bird-hide. In addition to the resident population, migratory ospreys are a regular feature of spring and autumn passage.

Rarities observed over the years have included bittern, great skua, great grey shrike and water pipit, and vagrants from southern Europe have included the exotic hoopoe and roller. Winter and early spring is also the best time to see flocks of the impressive crossbill stripping and devouring the seeds of conifer cones and it is a good practice to listen for mobile flocks flying over the road. Flocks of redwing and fieldfare are winter visitors only to suitable areas, along with brambling, which are invariably found with flocks of chaffinch.

The management of the lake and surrounding area is vital to the continued success of the ospreys. It was a culmination of several years' hard work by the Lake District Osprey partnership that finally resulted in the successful breeding of a pair of ospreys at Bassenthwaite in

2001 and ospreys have successfully nested ever since. Unfortunately overgrazing, invading plant and fish species, pollution and erosion threaten the fragile habitat of Bassenthwaite. The Bassenthwaite Lake Restoration Programme has been set up to do something about these problems. The partners working to protect the lake include Natural England, the Environment Agency, Forestry Commission, National Trust and United Utilities. The consortium aims to sustain the attractiveness of the whole of Bassenthwaite Lake, with its combination of open water, woodland, swamp, fen, marshy grasslands and lake edge.

Wonderful Wastwater

Meadow pipit

A bird watching challenge at 'the favourite view in the UK'

Start and finish: The village of Nether Wasdale at the southern end
of Wastwater
Grid Ref: NY129038
Distance: 5 miles (8km)
Time: Four to five hours
Grade: Easy to moderate
General: Several scattered hotels in the area provide toilet
and refreshment facilities. There are also adequate
facilities at the nearest villages of Ravenglass and
Gosforth

THE THREE-MILE LONG WASTWATER is England's deepest and perhaps most
enigmatic lake. On its eastern shore the famous screes below Illgill Head
come right down to the edge of the water. The lake nestles in the spectacular
valley of Wasdale, at the northern end of which are the dramatic mountains
of Yewbarrow, Kirkfell, Great Gable, Scafell Pike and Scafell, in all their
magnificent glory. All of this led to thousands of television viewers choosing
Wastwater as Britain's official favourite view. Set amid such breathtaking
scenery, why not exploit the bird watching potential by taking a circular walk
well off the beaten track and record all the species you see?

With certain exceptions most of the glacial lakes occupy depressions cut
by glaciers and dammed by moraines. They are too deep sided and lack
sufficient food on their pebbly shores to attract a great variety of birds,
including wildfowl, until frost drives them from shallower lakes and tarns.
To be honest the birding is good but not always that good, especially in
high summer, though the dramatic scenery may compensate any lack of
birds. The Wastwater challenge is for the walker to complete a five-mile

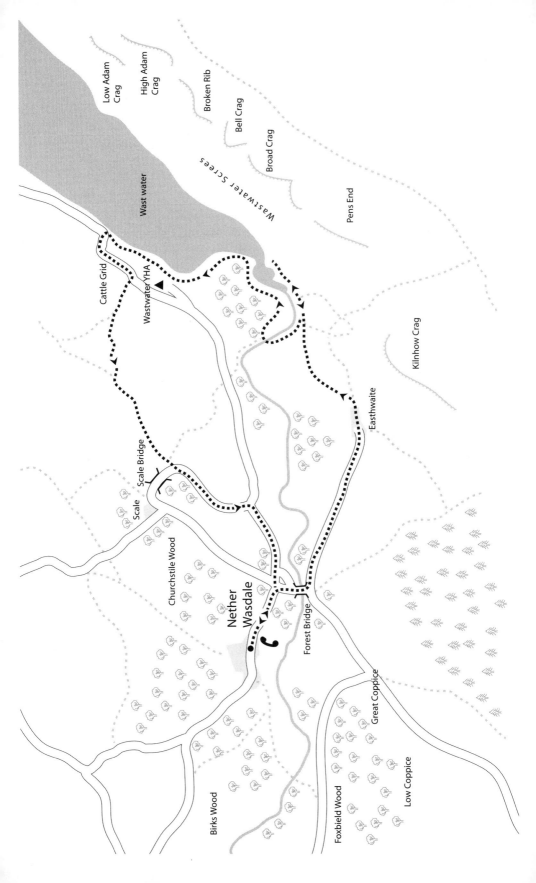

Low Adam Crag

High Adam Crag

Broken Rib

Bell Crag

Broad Crag

Wastwater Screes

Wast water

Pens End

Kilnhow Crag

Cattle Grid

Wastwater YHA

Scale Bridge

Scale

Churchstile Wood

Easthwaite

Nether Wasdale

Forest Bridge

Birks Wood

Foxfield Wood

Great Coppice

Low Coppice

walk commencing and finishing at Nether Wasdale, and to record the birds to be seen without any guidance as to likely species to be seen. A careful and observant approach in late April or early May should reveal one or two surprises – there was even a golden eagle seen hereabouts several decades ago but don't count on it today! In the meantime keep ceaseless watch for around forty probable suspects.

🚶 **Walk along the road from Nether Wasdale in the direction of the lake, forking right at the first junction at the road signposted Santon Bridge. After crossing a bridge over the River Irt, take the signed footpath to Wastwater that utilises the road to Easthwaite Farm. Pass the farm buildings and fork left towards the River Irt; thence follow the river to the edge of the stupendous 550-metre high screes to witness the awesome range of England's highest mountains at the head of the lake.**

🚶 **Follow the path back to reach Lund Bridge. Cross over the bridge and immediately thereafter pass through a kissing gate on the right into interesting mixed woodland habitat. Turn right and walk along a permissive path along the north side of the river before reaching the lakeshore. After passing a small boathouse there are more unfolding views of the mountains. Keep right following the lakeside and cross over a stile onto the road. Turn left onto the metalled road, being cautious of the traffic and walk a short distance along it to a footpath sign on the right. Take the rough track indicated to where trees on the left-hand side taper out. Here pass through a gate stile and look out for a faint grassy path veering first left and then right to reach a distinct bridleway. Turn left and follow the bridleway, ignoring the footpath sign to Woodhow. At the next junction follow the grassy track towards Galesyke to again reach the public road. Turn right here while again exercising caution around traffic before returning to the starting point at Nether Wasdale.**

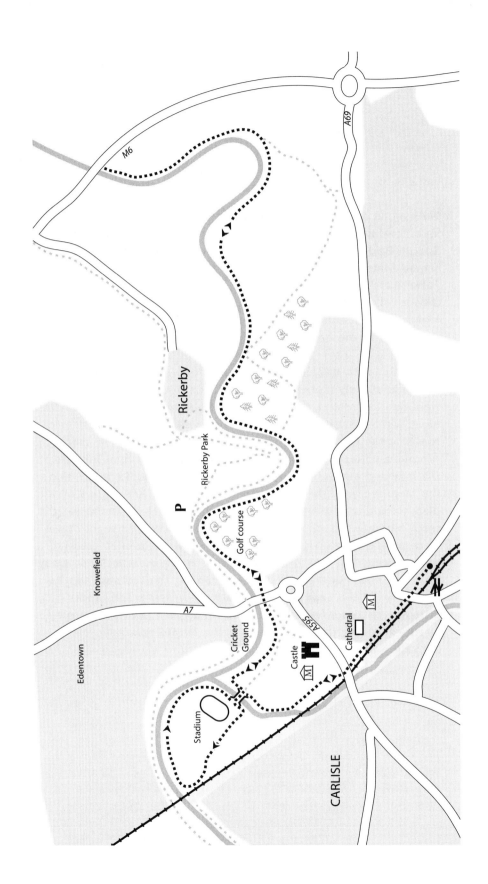

A Carlisle pathway to Eden

Sedge Warbler

Start and finish: Any convenient point in Carlisle City centre

Distance: Dependent on how far you want to walk, suggest a minimum of three miles

Time: Allow approximately five hours for the complete return walk from Caledonian Bridge to the M6 motorway crossing of the River Eden

Grade: Easy

General: Refreshments, toilet and parking facilities in and around Carlisle city centre. Sections of this walk are suitable for the disabled (PT)

T HE RIVER EDEN RISES in the hills above Cumbria's Mallerstang Common, about seventy miles upriver from Carlisle, and flows through the centre of the city to become the Solway Firth. Carlisle is one of Britain's oldest cities and dominates the borders between England and Scotland. Indeed its history goes back to the Romans who built a settlement here to serve the newly built Hadrian's Wall. The described riverside walk is easily accessible from the city centre and has been selected because it supports a surprisingly good and varied bird life throughout the year. The walk embraces parkland, a golf course, rough grazing land, meadow, trees and shrubs and, of course, the river. Thus it is ideal for foreign ornithologists visiting the city who may want to see a range of British birds, including the outside possibility of a rarity.

There are convenient car parks situated at The Sands Centre and in Rickerby Park. Alternatively for those arriving by train, walk along the Roman wall, past the cathedral and castle to Bitts Park and commence the walk at the Caledonian Railway bridge.

The riverside walk is along an easy, well-defined path which is situated on the south side of the Eden. Depending on the starting and finishing point, the distance/permutations of the walk are left to the walker's discretion. Carlisle is at the confluence of three rivers, the Eden, Caldew and Petteril, and the first river we reach is the Caldew, which is crossed by a footbridge.

(🚶) The Eden path continues between the river and Bitt's Park to Eden Bridge, adjacent to The Sands entertainment complex. Go under the subway at Eden Bridge and rejoin the river at The Sands. Continue to Rickerby Park suspension bridge and regain the riverside path alongside the golf course, crossing a footbridge over the River Petteril before arriving at the eastern extremity of the greens. Leaving the golf course one can now begin to hear the perpetual noise from the M6 and see the viaduct that crosses the Eden. However, do not be put off, simply follow the path alongside the now meandering river with green fields on either side while heading towards the viaduct. At a convenient point retrace your steps along the same route to the city centre.

🛈 The first stretch of river is the haunt of cormorant, heron, tufted duck, goosander, mallard, grey and pied wagtails. Keep watch on the river for all creatures great and small, including the elusive little grebe. This cute water bird and its larger relative, the great crested grebe, are sometimes to be seen swimming along the calmer stretches of the river. After crossing the bridge over the River Caldew, parkland habitat supports great spotted woodpecker, wood pigeon, bullfinch, chaffinch, greenfinch, goldfinch, robin, house sparrow, starling, blackbird, song thrush, mistle thrush, dunnock, treecreeper, wren, long-tailed, blue, great and coal tits.

The section of the walk from Eden Bridge is particularly productive, especially in spring time when warblers may be detected on song from deep inside the thick foliage of trees, shrubs and abundant riverside flora. Enjoy 'warbler alley,' where an abundance of willow warblers proclaim the arrival of spring with a descending cascade of notes. The scrub is especially good for this species, which arrives shortly after the chiffchaff, whose distinctive 'chiff-chaff, chiff-chaff' song emanates from the higher trees. Blackcaps also sing, but only a trained ear will distinguish their song from that of the garden warbler. Sedge warblers take advantage of the dense thickets of sallow while engaged in intermittent and often longer song cycles, and whitethroats sing their rather scratchy song from scattered bushes and low cover.

In addition reed bunting, goldfinch, linnet, lesser redpoll and the ubiquitous wren are all likely to be observed. The golf course is worth checking for oystercatcher, carrion crow, jackdaw, mistle thrush, meadow pipit and several species of gull. At one point the footpath crosses over a short section of the course so take care! Close to the river the banded demoiselle (*calyoptrex splendens*) is likely to add a splash of colour to the walk.

During the summer flocks of that superb master of flight, the swift, as well as swallow, house martin and sand martin, hunt for insects over the water. The latter species nests in the sandy river bank, as does one of our most strikingly colourful and well-known birds, the kingfisher. There is a very good chance of seeing a brilliant flash of blue flying low over the river at any point on this walk. Better still a kingfisher may be seen alighting onto a convenient post or overhanging branch while showing off their classic combination of colourful plumage, long bill and bedazzling red legs.

In the remnants of substantial meadows, some of which have now been transformed for agricultural use, listen and watch for skylarks, for at the time of writing it was still possible to enjoy the unmistakable song flight over these areas. Also, a few lapwings and curlews continue to breed though with varying degrees of success in marginal remnant habitats, while nesting oystercatcher and common sandpiper are probably more successful in their chosen nest sites alongside the river.

If water levels are low, waders may be attracted to the exposed mud and shingle of the river, especially in summer and autumn, and passage migrants such as black tern, green sandpiper and black-tailed godwit are distinct possibilities. Surprisingly, even that outstandingly rare migrant the whiskered tern has occurred, and nowadays a migrating osprey is always a distinct possibility in spring or autumn. More commonly observed raptors include buzzard, kestrel and sparrowhawk. Throughout the year black-headed gulls gather in the fields and at the edge of the river together with great and lesser black-backed, herring and common gulls, and just occasionally the less common Mediterranean gull. During winter large flocks of wigeon, Canada and greylag geese, mute and whooper swans occur in the fields near the motorway.

Wherever there are large flocks of waders and grazing wildfowl the peregrine falcon is likely to create mayhem and in all probability will not be far away. Peregrines are now regularly seen throughout Lakeland including the most urbanised areas of Carlisle. On the return walk there will be renewed opportunities to catch up on some of the birds and perhaps an opportunity to spy an otter doing a spot of fishing anywhere along the Eden. Look carefully for tracks and spraints, ideally avoiding busy periods to be in with a remote chance of spotting this splendid mammal, invariably at some unearthly hour!

Discovering Eden

Stock Dove

Start and finish: The Duke's Head Inn, Armathwaite
Grid Ref: NY505461
Distance: 4–5 miles (6–8 km)
Time: Allow four hours
Grade: Easy
General: Parking, toilet and refreshment facilities at
Armathwaite (PT)

THIS IS AN EASY bird watching walk beginning and ending at the village of Armathwaite, which nestles on the banks of the River Eden in a valley that is well wooded and characterised by its soft red sandstone. The famous Settle to Carlisle railway line, often described as England's most scenic main line railway, serves Armathwaite. The 72-mile long spectacular railway has seventeen major viaducts and seventeen tunnels and opened at the peak of Victorian railway construction in 1876. Comfortable modern trains run between Leeds and Carlisle seven days a week through the heart of the Yorkshire dales and the Eden valley, so why not enhance the day by taking the train to Armathwaite station?

Regardless of the method of transportation this walk commences at the Duke's Head Inn in the village centre. Nearby is a road bridge across the Eden and upstream there are views of Armathwaite Castle, with its Pele tower bearing witness to the Scottish border raids of the fifteenth and sixteenth centuries. Close by, the Eden flows through a spectacular red sandstone gorge and careful scrutiny yields a nineteenth-century folly of several faces carved into the sandstone. The carvings are low down on the banks of the river and for safety reasons their approach must never be contemplated when the river is in spate or if there is a likelihood of dangerous surges in water levels.

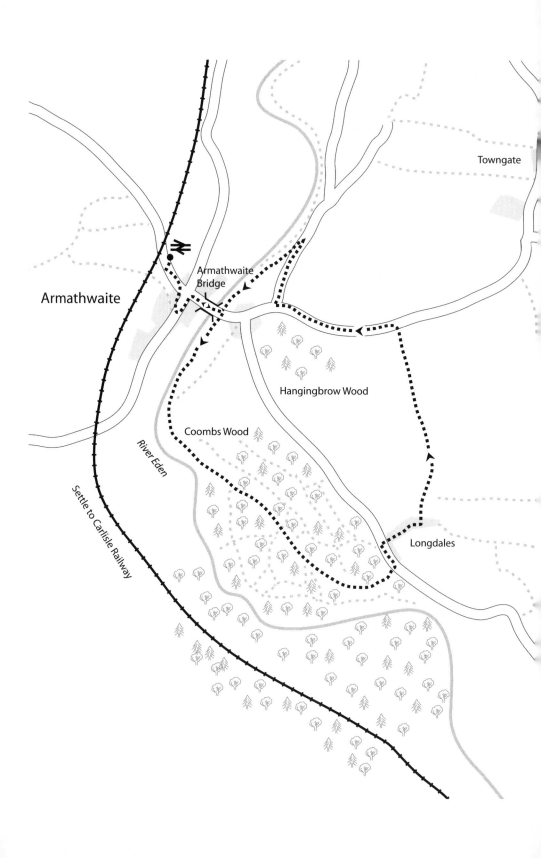

Towngate

Armathwaite
Bridge

Armathwaite

River Eden

Settle to Carlisle Railway

Hangingbrow Wood

Coombs Wood

Longdales

(𝔁) **Cross over the Eden Bridge and, just before reaching the Dog and Pheasant pub, descend the stone steps adjacent to the bridge to turn left under it to gain the riverbank. Walk upstream to a weir and salmon leap alongside a restored water mill on the opposite side of the river. At this point turn left into Coomb's Wood and right along the main footpath – a wide track that transects the woodland. Take the main track as it contours around the slope through the larch and mature pine trees, with fine views of the meandering river below. As the woodland tapers out you will eventually reach a gate and stile leading onto a road at Coomb head.**

ⓘ The walk is exhilarating throughout the seasons but is probably at its best in April and May when a heartening chorus of bird song enhances the rural scene. Around the village of Armathwaite the leading songsters are blackbird, song thrush, chaffinch, greenfinch, dunnock, robin, while not forgetting the chirpings of the familiar house sparrow and starling. Collared doves seem to call incessantly and the repetitive song of the wood pigeon is a great harbinger of spring. Great spotted woodpeckers may be recognised by their bouncing flight as they visit gardens from the nearby woodlands. House martins and swifts are invariably present, taking up residence in or upon local houses. These endearing summer visitors, along with the resident house sparrow and starling, are now given high conservation status and, to redress the balance of diminishing populations, they should ideally be given free accommodation whenever they seek it. Flocks of jackdaws are predominant around the village and in the extensive green fields and rural communities that are such a feature of the tranquil Eden Valley.

It is worth looking from the Eden Bridge for heron, mallard, goosander, dipper, grey and pied wagtail, and not forgetting that little gem of a bird, the kingfisher. Common sandpipers are summer visitors and are quite at home on this river. A sight to behold during autumn is that of the salmon vaulting up the salmon leap alongside the weir. The tree-lined river and adjacent Coomb's Wood should be scanned for siskin, lesser redpoll, gold crest, treecreeper and wandering flocks of long-tailed tit, as well as great, blue and coal tits. The raucous call and white rump of the jay are frequently all that can be heard and seen of this species as it flees into the woods that line the Eden.

Coomb's wood is an extensive and mature plantation managed by the Forestry Commission. It is pleasing to know that at the time of writing a few red squirrels may still be seen in these woods if you are lucky. Only time will tell if the reds are not to be permanently displaced by the errant and increasingly dominant alien grey squirrel that is now well established in many areas of Lakeland, including Coomb's Wood. Mammalian interest here features populations of badgers, fox, red and roe deer, contrasting with the smallest orders of mammal which include wood mouse, common shrew and the tiniest of all, the pygmy shrew.

Woodland birds should be looked for from the main track, while the steep, inaccessible woodland terrain lining the Eden is best left for nature. Typical birds of Coomb's wood include wren, goldcrest, chiffchaff, blackcap, willow warbler, bullfinch, chaffinch, redstart, green and great spotted woodpecker, spotted and pied flycatcher. Sadly, pied flycatchers have declined here despite the extensive provision of nest boxes throughout the woodland. Conversely, the nuthatch has increased significantly over the last two decades, and its vocal prowess usually belies its sedentary presence in this woodland, which until recently marked the northern limit of the nuthatch in England. Check larch and pine trees for they are likely to attract flocks of crossbills, especially when large numbers irrupt from the continent during so-called 'crossbill invasions'. Flocks of siskins and lesser redpolls sometimes fly over the open spaces and forest edge, and sparrowhawks come out of the spruce thickets to hunt along hedgerows and gardens.

🚶 **At the end of the woodland walk turn left then take the first minor road right, signposted to the hamlet of Longdales. After a short distance the tarmac road ends at the last house on the left. Turn left here and walk along a well-defined grassy track. Continue along the tree-lined path until it gradually descends to reach a road junction. Turn left then first right along a road signposted to Holmwrangle. (Alternatively, if tired or the weather is inclement, then advantage may be taken of a direct shorter route back to Armathwaite along the main road.) To continue the complete walk proceed towards Holmwrangle for about 300 metres to reach a public footpath sign on the left. Cross the stile and follow the path to the riverbank. Proceed to Armathwaite Bridge and the end of the walk.**

ℹ️ On the return leg of the walk the farming landscape is dominated by the meandering Eden and lowland valley pasture that harbour flocks of greylag and Canada geese. Gradually you reach elevated ground bisecting farmland and with excellent views of the Eden Valley and the route of Settle to Carlisle Railway line as it crosses one of its numerous Victorian viaducts. From the broad path that gradually descends into the valley one can look down onto soaring birds of prey, including buzzards and sparrowhawks. During winter roving flocks of redwings and fieldfares are fairly regular in trees and hedgerows in their relentless search for a good crop of berries. Look out for stock doves which nest in holes in trees and farm buildings, and which may be seen feeding and flying over arable fields. The curlew, with its long down-curved bill, is easily recognised as it flies over while demonstrating its splendid and evocative repertoire. Sadly, along with the attractive lapwing (formerly present here), it has suffered due to changes in agricultural practice.

Conversely, oystercatchers first started nesting on inland rivers such as the Eden over fifty years ago. Nowadays they are fairly abundant and may typically be seen perching on rocks or shingle banks while loudly flexing their strident vocal chords. A danger likely to befall them is a sudden spate of water, though eggs are usually laid where the beach is highest. In the winter the quieter stretches of the Eden are the haunt of diving ducks, including flocks of goosander and goldeneye. With luck they might be observed from a row of picturesque oak trees lining the river.

At the bridge the circular walk is complete, so why not ascend the stone steps to reach either one of two hostelries serving food and cask beer? After a modicum of refreshment a short walk at dusk along the riverbank towards Coomb's Wood might be rewarding – depending on the quantity of cask beer consumed! Tawny owls may be calling and in spring time woodcocks perform a haunting territorial 'roding' flight accompanied by bizarre croaking and 'click, click' calls.

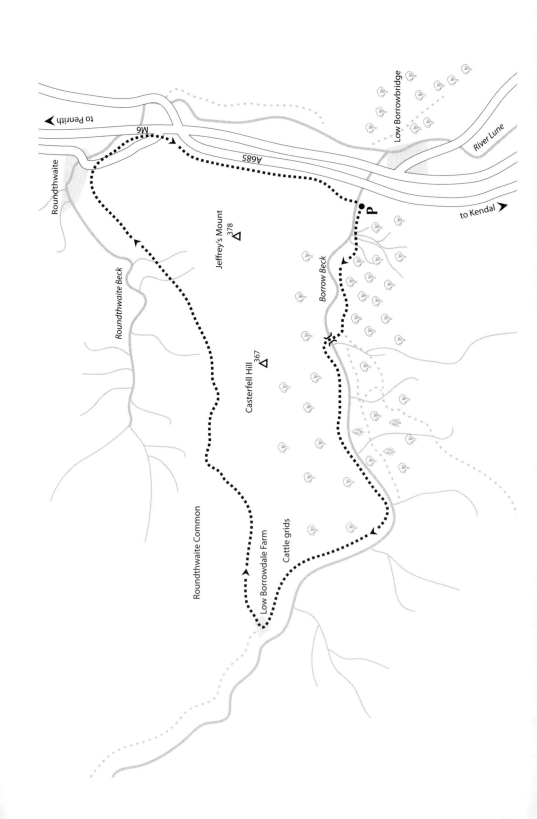

to Penrith

M6

Roundthwaite

Roundthwaite Beck

A685

Jeffrey's Mount
378

Casterfell Hill
367

Roundthwaite Common

Low Borrowdale Farm

Cattle grids

Borrow Beck

Low Borrowbridge

River Lune

to Kendal

P

Borrow Beck, Tebay

Dipper

Start: Small car park off the A785 at start of the Borrow
Beck Valley
Grid Ref: NY607015
Distance: 5 miles (8 km)
Grade: Moderate up to Low Borrowdale Farm.
General: Toilets, refreshments and shops in Tebay or
Westmorland Services on the M6

THIS SMALL ATTRACTIVE VALLEY off the Lune gorge is very typical of
many other Lakeland hill valleys. It is an easy walk through pleasant
countryside giving gentle bird watching throughout the year, although best
in the spring and early summer. This is quite a popular spring walk for bird
watching groups.

**From the car park follow the good track through the woodland
and up the valley to the bridge across the beck.**

Typical woodland birds such as long-tailed tit, treecreeper and green
and great spotted woodpeckers occur in numbers in the first part of
the woodland. As the trees thin, look out for tree pipit, wheatear and
redstart. Willow warblers become abundant in the more open areas
along with one or two pairs of spotted flycatchers. Where there are
small copses of mature trees pied flycatchers and nuthatch occur, while
higher up the hill away from the track curlews can be heard giving their
lovely 'bubbling' call; later in the season they call anxiously to warn the
young of your approach. Goldcrests and coal tits occur mainly around
the few remaining conifers. Birds of prey include buzzard, sparrowhawk

and kestrel. An evening visit in spring can often be rewarded with
calling tawny owls or even the sight of a barn owl hunting the fields
or fellside. Then, as dusk approaches, woodcock perform their ghostly
'roding' flight up and down the valley.

For much of the first part of this section the path is a little distance
away from the beck, but as you approach the bridge listen out for the
high, ringing call of the common sandpiper. This summer visitor is at
home on most fast-flowing streams. Easily identified from its crouched
posture and the constant rocking of its rear body, its flight is also
distinctive, with rapid, shallow wing beats as it flits between rocks or
across the water. When young are present it becomes quite agitated,
calling incessantly and objecting to your presence. Dippers and grey
wagtails are also regular breeders. Grey wagtails tend to move out in
winter to find less arduous conditions along the coast or further south
but dippers remain even during the severest of frosts.

⊛ **Follow the track alongside the stream to the isolated farm of
Low Borrowdale. Most groups retrace their steps from here
back to the car park but a circular walk back to the car park is
possible crossing upland pasture. From Low Borrowdale take the
signposted track over Roundthwaite Common and on to the hamlet
of Roundthwaite, then down the track and back along the A685 to
the car park.**

❶ The typical stream-side birds described above occur all the way up
to the farm. They are joined by swallows hawking insects over the
water. The steeper bracken-strewn slopes with patches of scrub attract
stonechat and whitethroats. Yellowhammers have been recorded in
small numbers recently.

The rushy fields of Roundthwaite Common hold a good population
of curlew and in the wetter areas lapwing and snipe. The call of the
male snipe has two very distinct and totally different ways of declaring
his territory or displaying to his mate. The first and most spectacular
is the so-called drumming; although birds can 'drum' at any time of
the day early mornings and evenings are best. After drumming the
male often lands on a post or occasionally a stone wall and gives
a loud vocal 'chip chip chip' to further establish his territory. When
flushed the bird rises suddenly and leaves with a zigzag, pitching flight
accompanied by a rather harsh scraping note.

Meadow pipits and skylarks are abundant and their contrasting song
flights make an interesting comparison. The well-known ascending
outpouring of the skylark, often continued for up to fifteen minutes at

a time, contrasts with the simple and brief song flight of the meadow pipit which is over in a few seconds.

In winter birds are scarce on these open habitats, most of the breeding birds moving to the coast or further south. However, some raptors move in, including occasional short-eared owl, hen harrier and merlin. The main prey are probably small mammals and the large flocks of starlings.

In spring and summer on the approach to the hamlet of Roundthwaite watch out for swallows, house martins and swifts. It is quite a thought that these three species are totally dependent on man for their nesting sites and have obviously benefited enormously from man's activities. Recently, however, with the advent of plastic fascias and general renovation and conversion of houses many former nesting sites have been lost.

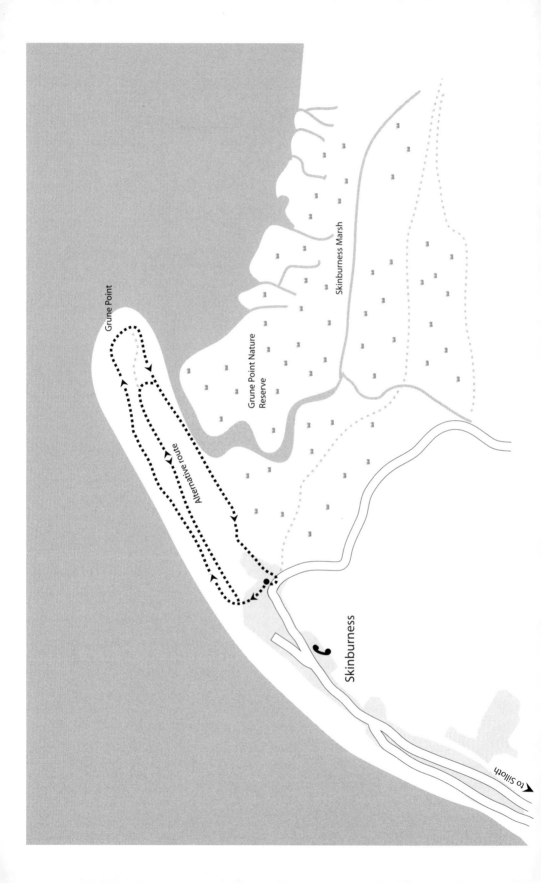

Grune Point

Grune Point Nature
Reserve

Skinburness Marsh

Alternative route

Skinburness

to Silloth

Grune Point, Silloth on Solway

Knot

Start and finish: Skinburness Road (B5302) at its junction with
Dicktrod Lane, Skinburness (PT)

Grid Ref: NY128561

Distance: 3 miles (4.8 km)

Time: Four hours

Grade: Easy

General: Toilet, parking and refreshment facilities at Silloth.
An hourly bus service from Maryport to Silloth and
Skinburness serves the starting point of the walk.
Part of the walk overlooking Skinburness Marsh
is suitable for the disabled. A visit to the Silloth
Discovery Centre is recommended (telephone
01697331944)

W HILE EN ROUTE TO Silloth from the south it is of note that the scenic
coastal road from Maryport passes alongside Allonby Bay, where there
is much to interest the naturalist. Yellow horned poppy, sea holly and the Isle
of Man cabbage adorn the sand dunes, while further inland there are thriving
clumps of thrift, sea campion and sea plantain. At Beckfoot, just south of
Silloth, you can park and watch the flocks of wildfowl and waders feeding at
high tide. Several years ago a hoopoe was found in a garden at Beckfoot and
although there is no guarantee that this exotic Mediterranean visitor will put
in another appearance, you could just be lucky.

Silloth on Solway, like so many other towns and villages, was first developed
with the opening of the railway on the 28 August, 1856. Almost inevitably a
certain Dr Beeching issued the line with a prescription for closure and the
last passenger train ran along the single track to Carlise in 1964. Today

Silloth is an interesting Victorian town with superb views across the Solway Firth of Criffell and the mountains of Dumfries and Galloway. Of interest are the cobbled tree-lined streets and a plaque on the wall of the National Westminster Bank in Eden Street, stating that the renowned international contralto Kathleen Ferrier resided in the former town house during the late 1930s. Skinburness is situated at the northern extremity of suburban Silloth. In medieval times it was Edward I's naval supply base for his invasions of Scotland, but a severe storm destroyed the sea defences and thus the original old town in 1302. Five years later Edward I died on the Solway marshes within sight of the coveted Scottish mainland across the Firth.

(X) **On arrival at Skinburness Road walk along the unmade Dicktrod Lane to the promenade. Here a sign indicates 'public footpath around Grune Point'. Continue to follow the coastal footpath to where it reaches the beach and then walk across a short stretch of shingle. Regain the footpath and after passing an isolated house on the right keep left on the path bisecting swards of gorse to Grune Point. Walk round the point but stay on the path to avoid disturbing ground-nesting birds. Return to the centre of Skinburness village via a track that passes an old gun turret and Skinburness Marsh. To the north of Grune Point the Cumbria Coastal Way crosses the marsh and skirts Moricambe Bay – not to be confused with Morecambe Bay!**

ⓘ On this walk we explore the Grune Point peninsula at the northern end of Silloth. This happens to be one of the most enjoyable circular walks in Cumbria throughout the bird watching year. The Solway is vital for thousands of wildfowl and waders which occur in winter in sensational numbers.

The best time to do the walk is on a rising tide between September and April when wildfowl and waders make the Solway a focal point for migrant birds from far and wide. Migration is nothing short of a phenomenon, involving many species and countless individuals, and the main themes of this walk are bird migration and navigation, which we will attempt to explain and exemplify.

On arrival at Skinburness walk to the end of Dicktrod Lane and scan the Solway Firth in all directions. The Solway is something of an international crossroads, ranking highly in the top ten of wader haunts in official censuses, with large numbers of knot, dunlin, curlew, oystercatcher, turnstone, redshank, grey plover, golden plover, lapwing, ringed plover and declining numbers of sanderling and bar-tailed godwit. The term 'passage migrant' generally describes birds that pass through the country twice a year while migrating from a breeding area further north, for example Scandinavia, and winter quarters further south, usually in Africa. During spring and autumn the following passage waders are possible candidates: little stint, spotted redshank, whimbrel, common sandpiper, green sandpiper, wood sandpiper and curlew sandpiper. Waders flying up the estuary at low tide to feed on a rich harvest of invertebrates in the intertidal areas of the Firth make a fine sight and are best seen an hour or two before high tide, before they fly off to favoured high tide roosts. Several thousand knot and masses of golden plover congregate on the marshes of Moricambe Bay on the Solway Estuary during late autumn.

Grune Point and the approaches to it comprise a mixture of interesting habitats with hawthorn hedgerows and extensive strands of gorse with open grassy areas. The varied habitat supports resident stonechat, linnet, skylark, meadow pipit, goldfinch, greenfinch, song thrush, reed bunting and in summer willow warbler, whitethroat and wheatear. Autumn passage and winter brings goldcrest, redstart and the possibility of a rare visitor such as a wintering snow bunting or shore lark that visited the point during the 1990s. During the spring and summer oystercatcher, ringed plover and certain other species may be found nesting on the extensive areas of pebbles surrounding Grune Point. Their eggs are wonderfully camouflaged to match their surrounding, but the effectiveness of this disguise can also be their undoing as a single careless footstep on what is seemingly unimportant shingle can be disastrous. For this reason it is very important to stay on the path and if you see a ringed plover feigning injury by drooping a wing avoid the area completely.

Flocks of black-headed and common gulls languish on the estuary and, given the right season and weather conditions, expect to see offshore kittiwake and little gull. Rare winter visitors have included Sabine's, glaucous and Iceland gulls. During spring and summer Sandwich, Arctic, common and little terns are regularly seen off Grune Point.

Great crested grebes are regular on the sea, though conversely red-necked and black-necked grebe are less frequent. Spring and autumn can be good for red-throated divers, and indeed great northern and black-throated diver should not be discounted. During autumn and winter separate rafts of wildfowl feature red-breasted merganser, scaup, mallard, goldeneye, teal and large flocks of wigeon and pintail. Moricambe Bay is an important site for wildfowl but sadly the last of the Solway punt gunners still strike terror into their midst. Away from their normal haunts at Rockliffe marsh and their Scottish base on the north bank of the Solway at Caelavarock and Merse Farm, thousands of barnacle and pink-footed geese may be seen in and around Moricambe Bay between November and March. They may be joined by flocks of whooper swans from Iceland. Young swans or cygnets are said to migrate with their parents on their first trip, which is presumably to learn the route. How then do birds like the whooper swans and barnacle geese find their way from one country to another, often ending up at exactly the same site that they left several months previously?

At Grune Point many birds, including rarities, have been ringed to shed light onto the mysteries of bird migration, though it is a complex subject that has baffled scientists for years and we still don't know all the answers. Ornithological research, however, reveals that most birds use a combination of navigational skills. Migrating birds can pinpoint their route by the exact position of the sun at any hour. On clear nights birds also use the constellations to guide them. Once birds have reached the general area of their destination, they start to rely more on visual landmarks, such as rivers, hills and buildings, to help them home in on their final site. On their flight from Svalbard, for example, barnacle geese use a number of North Sea islands as resting and refuelling points. They are capable of crossing the North Sea – a distance of 480 kilometres or 300 miles – in just five hours. What is even more surprising is that birds have the equivalent of a built-in compass; for example, pigeons have a mineral called magnetite embedded in their skulls, which picks up the earth's magnetic forces. Amazingly the wonders of migration are said to extend to the birds perceiving the information that the magnetite provides as two bright spots in their vision, the intensity of each providing them with their directional clues.

Nevertheless migrating birds do sometimes get blown off course by bad weather and end up hopelessly lost. Exceptionally rare vagrants originating from three continents have been sighted at Grune Point over the years. These are represented by long-billed dowitcher, buff-breasted and pectoral sandpiper from North America, white stork, glossy ibis, squacco, night and purple heron, wryneck, bluethroat, Lapland bunting, golden oriole, red-backed shrike, barred and melodious warbler from central Europe and yellow-browed warbler from the steppes of Central Asia. Anything can turn up but care should always be exercised when observing tired migratory birds and the bird's individual welfare must always come first. Nevertheless it is the unpredictable element of what you might find that makes bird watching such a fascinating and intriguing pursuit.

Bowness-on-Solway

Snipe

Tranquility and birds aplenty

Start: Bowness-on-Solway
Grid Ref: NY232627
Distance: 5 miles (8 km)
Time: Depending on time of year allow five to eight hours for the walk
Grade: Easy
General: Toilet, restricted retail and refreshment facilities at Bowness-on-Solway

THE REMOTE VILLAGE OF Bowness-on-Solway is not adequately served by public transport and therefore it is better to use your own. Parts of the described walk are suitable for the disabled and there are also several lay-bys along the minor road that passes through Port Carlisle, Bowness-on-Solway, Cardurnock and Anthorn. Parking facilities along this road offer a range of locations to see waders and wildfowl but please be aware that on the highest tides the road can be submerged (marked by warning signs).

We start and finish this bird-watching walk at the quiet village of Bowness-on-Solway, situated to the north-east of Moricambe Bay, and it contrasts greatly, and should not be confused with, the tourist resort of Bowness on Windermere. It may be of interest to know that this walk commences at the start of the 81-mile long Hadrian's Wall National Trail, which runs to Wallsend in north-east England. At its Bowness-on-Solway western extremity there is little evidence of the Roman wall itself, however, although archaeologists have discovered exciting evidence about life here in Roman times – indeed stones from the wall can be found in some of the local buildings. You can explore Hadrian's Wall by using the seasonal Hadrian's Wall bus service that stops at visitor attractions along the route

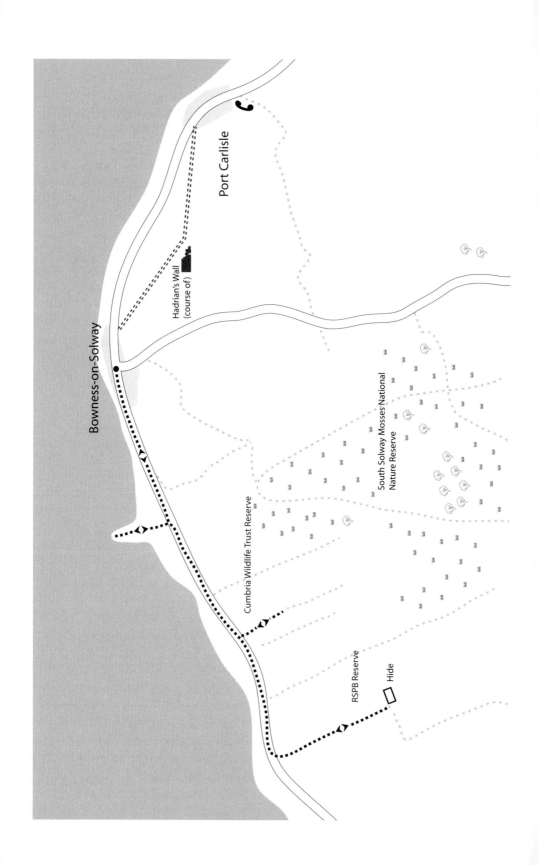

Bowness-on-Solway

Port Carlisle

Hadrian's Wall
(course of)

Cumbria Wildlife Trust Reserve

South Solway Mosses National
Nature Reserve

RSPB Reserve

Hide

between Carlisle and Hexham. A restricted bus service also operates from Carlisle to Bowness-on-Solway on certain days.

(人) **As far as the dedicated walk is concerned park either side of Bowness village where adequate parking facilities are provided. At the village centre follow the footpath signs to 'The Banks', where there is an excellent shelter overlooking the Solway. Walk west along the metalled road for about one mile to the remains of the Solway railway viaduct at Herdhill Scar (grid reference 213628). Gain the old railway embankment and walk as far as you can to the end to gain the best views of the Solway and its birds, but be warned that no right of way exists. Thereafter continue to walk west along the road to a gated track on the left with a sign indicating 'Bowness-on-Solway Nature Reserve'. Access can be gained via a farm track which bisects the reserve at grid reference 206617. Go left along the track to explore the reserve via a series of easy to follow paths before regaining the road and walking a further mile or so to Campfield Marsh Nature Reserve at North Plain Farm. Here a footpath should be taken to reach the RSPB hide. Retrace your steps back to Bowness-on-Solway along the same outward route, thus affording yet more opportunities to make some good sightings.**

ⓘ This is an excellent bird watching walk complemented by the backdrop of Crifell and the mountains of Dumfries and Galloway. The Solway Firth is a World Heritage Site, a European Marine Site and a Special Area of Conservation. The area around Bowness is festooned with nature reserves of international and local importance. On this particular walk we embrace the renowned skua-watching point on the Solway Firth and the local Cumbria Wildlife Trust Reserve of Bowness-on-Solway, as well as the RSPB's Campfield Marsh Nature Reserve at North Plain Farm, where parking facilities are provided (the reserve telephone number is 01697 351330, it is open at all times and admission is free).

As with all estuarine bird watching be aware of the state of the tide. Commence birding the minute you step out of the car and reach the shelter at 'The Banks'. You will find that this elevated facility is an excellent place to have a picnic while viewing the Firth, especially on a wet day. Either side of high tide offers the best opportunities to see shore birds. At low tide most waders feed on distant mudflats and any passage seabirds tend to be harder to find in the vast expanse of the Firth. Approach the shelter cautiously so as not to flush the more usual ringed plover, grey plover, oystercatcher, redshank and dunlin flocks. In autumn passage waders such as greenshank, curlew sandpiper and little stint may fly in to enhance these flocks.

During late winter and spring both the shelter and the extended promontory of the old railway viaduct (the most productive sea-watching point) can afford excellent views of various species of divers, auks, wildfowl, waders, terns, kittiwake and fulmar. In addition, any bird watcher will tell you that the spring passage of skuas at Bowness-on-Solway is one of the main events on the ornithological calendar. On reaching the remains of the viaduct that once linked England with Scotland some walkers choose to gain the embankment and walk to the end along a rough track to fully exploit an ornithological phenomenon. However, please be warned that this is not a public right of way and is overgrown in places so this is not included in the walk directions, the decision to deviate from the path being entirely yours.

The skua passage is especially pronounced between mid April and mid May and as always when birding exploit the right weather conditions. At Bowness south-westerly winds combined with showers/light rain are the best for a dedicated watch for all four species of skua, but especially for the migratory passage of pomarine and long-tailed skua. This weather condition usually funnels these birds into the Firth and keeps them low over the sea as they begin their overland flight to the North Sea and their ultimate destinations in the far north of Arctic Europe. Evidence that they use the 'Tyne Gap' is provided by skua records at various points along this confirmed migration route.

The viaduct is certainly the best place to see the pomarine skua, resplendent in spring plumage with its characteristic long, twisted, spoon-shaped tail. Total numbers can vary in any one year, usually between one hundred and six hundred birds. Smaller numbers of the elegant long-tailed skua, with their extraordinarily long, two central tail feathers projecting well beyond the other tail feather, also occur in flocks of up to around twenty birds. Witnessing the spring passage of skuas from this prominent vantage point can be an altogether awe-inspiring experience.

During winter, north-west winds bring rafts of scaup from their more usual haunts off the Scottish side of the Firth onto the south side, where they can usually be seen at various locations anywhere between Bowness and Silloth. As you walk along the road it soon becomes apparent that Campfield Marsh is one of the last areas to be partly submerged by the rising tide. Flocks of pintail, shelduck, wigeon, mallard and teal, with smaller offshore flocks of great crested grebe, goldeneye, goosander, and red breasted merganser, are all possibilities and are generally less dependent on the prevailing weather conditions. The area of marsh to the west of the RSPB's North Plain is used as a roosting area by wading birds such as oystercatcher, redshank, curlew, ringed, grey and golden plovers, dunlin, knot and turnstone, but these days, only a few bar-tailed godwit.

The Cumbria Wildlife Trust Reserve of Bowness-on-Solway, is situated one mile west of the village adjacent to Campfield Marsh. The easy-to-follow nature trail utilises boardwalks around a series of former gravel pits and supports an amazing variety of plant and animal life. Owing to possible flooding parts of the trail are not to be recommended during wet weather. The varying depths of the pools provide a good habitat for mallard, heron and moorhern and for many species of dragonflies and damselflies, including red, common and ruddy darter, common hawker dragonflies, and azure, common blue, blue-tailed and emerald damselflies. The ponds have their own special flora and are used by both smooth and great crested newts, as well as by large numbers of frogs and toads. The common lizard is often to be found basking in the sun and may even share a wooden seat with you!

The maturing willow and hawthorn scrub and strands of gorse provide valuable food and shelter for many species of breeding birds, including bullfinch, greenfinch, linnet, whitethroat, willow warbler, blackcap, sedge warbler and other warblers. Willow tit can still be found here close to the extreme edge of its British range in Dumfries and Galloway. Listen for the distinctive 'pee-pee-pee' calls, usually a give away. Sadly this little bird is quietly disappearing from many of its English haunts and one can only speculate as to the complex factors governing its demise. Nevertheless the degeneration of suitable woodland habitat and nesting sites are probably at the forefront.

The botanist will find much to delight in the ungrazed, flower-rich grassland represented by twenty-three varieties of grass. There are cushions of yellow tormentil, silverweed, speedwell, heath bedstraw, knapweed, swathes of common and northern marsh orchids, and marsh pennywort, with round leaves the size of an old penny. The abundance of flowers, especially knapweed, naturally attracts butterflies. In summer these include ringlet, small tortoiseshell, peacock, red admiral, wall brown, meadow brown, large skipper and small copper butterflies. Overall this is a very pleasant reserve so just relax and enjoy the rich biodiversity on offer before moving on to the contrasting bird reserve that is Campfield Marsh.

Campfield Marsh Reserve is made up of a mosaic of different habitats comprising saltmarsh, peatbogs, farmland and wet grassland. The reserve includes parts of Bowness Common Site of Special Interest as well as the Upper Solway Flats and Marshes Site of Special Scientific Interest. The lowland raised peat bog, or raised mire, is a rare wildlife habitat that is particularly important for invertebrates and plant life and for one of the last-remaining lowland populations of the red grouse in the UK, though on this particular walk it is extremely unlikely that you will see one.

On entering the reserve at Northfield Farm check the kale field for tree sparrows and observe the strategically placed nest boxes for several breeding pairs. During spring and summer the reserve provides a sanctuary for tree sparrow and skylark and other diminishing species, thanks to an enlightened conservation programme. A total of seventy-five species have bred here. Farmland management work aims to restore the natural wet conditions that occurred here before parts of this habitat were drained for agriculture.

In fields close to the hide snipe may be seen feeding before flying off with characteristic zigzag flight and harsh calls. The snipe is a highly secretive wader that is usually seen after being flushed. However, at this site it can still be seen and heard as it displays over its territory while creating a 'drumming' sound with its outer tail feathers. Grazing cattle and sheep provide the habitat for wading birds to breed and numbers of snipe, lapwing, curlew and redshank are quite successful. For example, in 2009 there were seventeen pairs of snipe, seven pairs of redshank and fifteen pairs of curlew nesting on the reserve. Other non-breeding waders occur and in spring golden plovers really live up to their name when they show off their stunning spangled black and gold breeding plumage.

Throughout the changing seasons many species of birds may be seen from the screens and the excellent hide. Uncommon migrants are not without precedent and both osprey and spoonbill are known to occur from time to time. There are also well-documented accounts of American vagrants, including long-billed dowitcher, American wigeon and American and Pacific golden plovers. In winter wigeon, shoveler, pintail and teal gather on the flooded farm fields in good numbers; in fact over 1% of the UK's teal population spend the winter at Campfield Marsh and thousands of pink-footed and barnacle geese feed on the farmland and salt marshes. At dusk whooper swans flight onto the fields to roost. Hen harrier may be seen flying slowly over the ground, hunting for small birds and mammals. Males are superb, with their pale grey plumage and black wing tips, while the female is mainly brown with a conspicuous white rump. Other species of raptors and owls may also be present, including short-eared owl and barn owl. The short-eared owl is one of the few species of owl that can be seen during daylight hours and is a specialist hunter of voles, with numbers fluctuating dramatically during 'good' vole years. With such rich pickings to be had it is good to relax and enjoy this entirely free ornithological trail as many times as you want. Doubtless you will not find all of the aforementioned interesting creatures and birds, although you might find a few new ones – good hunting!

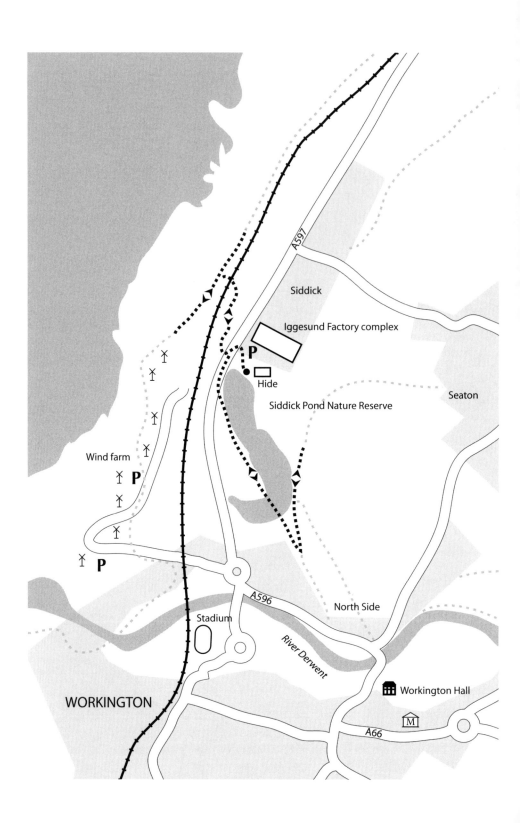

A597

Siddick

Iggesund Factory complex

P

Hide

Siddick Pond Nature Reserve

Seaton

Wind farm

P

P

A596

North Side

Stadium

River Derwent

Workington Hall

M

A66

WORKINGTON

Siddick Ponds

Great crested grebe

An ornithological oasis near Workington

Start and finish: Iggesund Paper Board's main car park, Siddick, Workington (PT). A bird hide is situated a few metres from car park and is suitable for the disabled. However, the walk along the shore is unsuitable for wheelchairs

Grid Ref: NY000309

Distance: 2.1 miles (3.3 km)

Time: Four to five hours

Grade: Easy

General: Siddick Ponds Nature Reserve is situated north of the River Derwent and east of the A596, two miles north of Workington. There are no toilet or retail facilities at the reserve; the nearest are situated at Workington or Maryport town centre. The area is served by railway stations at Workington and Maryport and a regular bus service that passes the entrance to the reserve at Siddick

THIS WALK EMBRACES THE Siddick Pond local nature reserve with an option to incorporate the tidal foreshore for waders and seabirds. The complete walk around the reserve and foreshore is approximately three miles, depending on how much of the foreshore is covered by the walker.

🚶 **Visitors arriving by car are welcome to use the car park within the Iggesund factory complex next to the reserve. On arrival all visitors should report at the security office and obtain a key for the bird hide.**

❶ Curiously hidden amid towering wind farms, modern industrial large retail establishments blended with slag heaps, and old railway tracks that serve as constant reminders of the area's industrial past, is an ornithological oasis known as Siddick Ponds. In fact this local nature reserve is a legacy of the iron ore industry and its association with the first railways of the Victorian era. Siddick Pond was created in 1870 when a depression was first excavated in order to build the railways that served the mines. The site was formerly a horse-racing course known as the sea gate or 'sigget,' hence the origin of the name. Over a period of 140 years the marsh has developed to form the present mosaic of habitats, ranging from open water, reed swamp, rough grassland and scrub.

Siddick Ponds reserve is today an important wildlife site and a good example of a particularly scarce habitat along the industrialised west Cumbrian coast, factors that led to its being declared a Site of Special Scientific Interest in 1951 and a local nature reserve managed by Allerdale Borough Council in 1951. The reed beds feature the common reed and provide food, shelter and nest sites for many characteristic species, while the reserve as a whole has a variety of breeding, passage and wintering birds totalling over 170 species. The abandoned railway line embankments serve as a network of cycle tracks/footpaths and provide fine views of the reserve.

A quick glance at the logbook inside the hide will give you all the latest sightings. These records allude to all forms of wildlife, and usually feature sightings of the otter, well worth looking out for especially during the twilight hours. Further examination of the interpretive displays will reveal the diverse list of regular seasonal and uncommon migrant birds to be seen throughout the year.

Residents include black-headed and other species of gull that come to bathe. Cormorants are regular, together with the almost inevitable feral flocks of greylag geese and the odd heron or two. A high percentage of resident waterfowl breed in the reed beds and associated patches of mud, rush and sedge, which are a haven for little grebe, water rail, moorhen, coot, mute swan, mallard, shoveler, tufted duck and pochard – the latter at its only regular breeding site in Cumbria.

Late April and May is the best time to be in with a chance of seeing passage migrants and from time to time these may include migrating osprey, marsh harrier, garganey, black tern, little gull and wood sandpiper, not forgetting newly arrived flocks of swift and hirundines that skim low over the water for insects. Passerines of the reed bed and the peripheral areas of willow are represented by lesser redpoll, reed bunting, grasshopper warbler, willow warbler, sedge and reed warbler. It was as late as 1959 that a reed warbler's nest was first discovered at Siddick Ponds. Almost at the northern limit of their British breeding grounds, the reed warbler is now well established at this and several other specific sites in Cumbria.

In late summer many hirundines, mainly swallow, sand martin and house martin, roost in the reeds. As autumn progresses it is worth looking out for spotted redshank, little stint, curlew, sandpiper, ruff, greenshank, green sandpiper, black tern, pied flycatcher and warblers. The reserve is important for migratory birds following the coastline, and freshwater marshes near the coast such as this are always likely to attract seasonal rarities, although one wonders how the recent installation of innumerable giant wind turbines adjacent to the reserve will affect them. Nevertheless, birds far more unpredictable in their occurrence have included species as diverse as long-tailed skua, red-necked phalarope, spoonbill, hoopoe, nightjar, little bunting, savis, barred and yellow-browed warbler. Significantly, a flock of bearded tits irrupted into this area of Cumbria in both 1981 and 1990.

Between November and March the star attraction throughout several consecutive winters since 1992 has been the bittern. Check out the gulls, especially in winter, for glaucous or other white winged gulls. Commoner wildfowl, including wigeon, teal, shoveler, pochard, tufted duck, goldeneye, gadwall, pintail, red-breasted merganser, goosander, great crested grebe and flocks of coot, are often present. Following periods of gales at sea red-throated diver, black-necked grebe, scaup, common scoter, smew and the old squaw – better known in Britain as the long-tailed duck – have all occurred, although of course not on the same day!

During the winter months whooper swans occasionally join the mute swans and other wildfowl. Also during winter look out for kingfisher, grey wagtail and stonechat, for snipe on the mud fringed edges of reed, and its smaller cousin the jacksnipe might put in a celebrity appearance and perform its speciality act. Constant dipping movements while feeding are fascinating to watch and are a characteristic of this species. The reed bed is used by starlings, performing their own aerial spectacle by creating extraordinary shapes and patterns above the proposed roost site, in the absence of a reception committee of raptors, of course. Sparrowhawk are most often seen and peregrine and merlin occur more rarely. Barn owls may sometimes be present and there have also been sporadic sightings of tawny, short-eared and long-eared owls.

After your sojourn in the bird hide return the key to the office and consider walking to the shore and/or viewing the reserve from the railway embankments.

Ⓧ **To reach the shore turn right along the A596 past McGowan Street. Take the first footpath on the left that leads to the shore. Take care crossing over the main railway line via a pedestrian level crossing to gain the Cumbria Coastal way above the shore. Walk as far as you want in either direction along the Cumbria Coastal Way, taking care to avoid the potentially dangerous steep banks of slag spoil.**

ⓘ View the sea from the elevated Cumbrian Coastal Way path, avoiding the steeply graded slag heaps. On the beach there are usually flocks of cormorant, oystercatcher, curlew, redshank, ringed plover, great black-back gulls and other species of gull, which should be scanned for anything unusual. The state of the tide strongly influences what can be seen, especially during times of seasonal migration and in the winter months. When doing an organised sea watch anything is possible, ranging from rare skuas chasing the terns to a Ross's gull that was once recorded offshore at Workington. Depending on optimum weather conditions and the appropriate season watch the sea for any divers, grebes, kittiwake, fulmar, gannet, auks, Manx shearwater and kittiwake. Storm and Leach's petrel both occur off the Cumbrian coast during times of strong westerly gales, and the uncommon species of shearwaters should not be discounted. Also notable are flocks of offshore sea ducks of various species.

As you walk along the path adjacent to the shore look and listen out for meadow and rock pipit, for both are distinct possibilities. The rock pipit has a distinctive metallic 'phist phist call' while flying over the tide-line, where it feeds on the numerous flies which settle on the decaying weeds and picks up invertebrates from shallow pools. During winter care should also be taken with the identification of twite and linnet, for both species occur. One of the best aids to identification is to listen for their characteristic calls. This area of predominantly industrial waste, with plenty of emergent vegetation such as sea buckthorn and gorse, is also the haunt of meadow pipit, stonechat, raven and kestrel.

Ⓧ **To view the rest of Siddick Reserve retrace your steps back over the level crossing to join a footpath/cycle way that crosses over the A596 and then passes alongside the western side of the reserve where it can be viewed from the elevated embankment. At the southern end of the reserve a junction left affords good views of the eastern side of the reserve. After viewing, return to the car park and complete the walk.**

❶ The old railway embankments offer further opportunities to observe the rest of the reserve and any of the aforementioned species, as well as the otter. In addition the embankments are covered with bramble, gorse and mature hawthorns, ideal for breeding blackcap, whitethroat, lesser whitethroat, goldfinch and linnet.

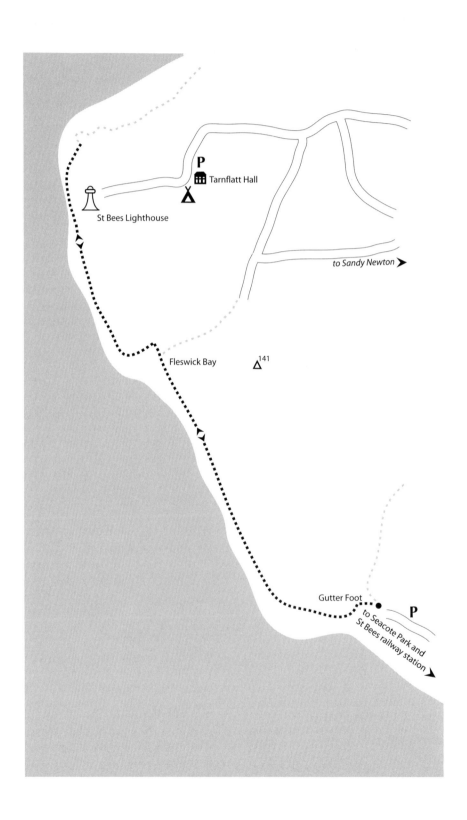

P

Tarnflatt Hall

St Bees Lighthouse

to Sandy Newton ❯

Fleswick Bay

△141

Gutter Foot

P

to Seacote Park and
St Bees railway station ❯

St Bees Head

Guillemot

Start: Car park at St Bees. This walk is easily accessible
from St Bees railway station

Grid Ref: NX961111

Grade: Easy to moderate

Distance: 5 miles (8 km)

General: Toilets and other facilities in St Bees (PT)

THIS RSPB RESERVE IS the only cliff nesting seabird colony in the north-west of England, and a visit at the height of the breeding season in May and June is a unique and unforgettable experience. The red sandstone cliffs, which rise to almost 300 feet, provide nesting sites for myriad seabirds. All species are visible from the cliff-top footpath, and the best sites have three specially constructed viewing platforms, allowing one to experience the constant activity and cacophony of sound (and smell) of a seabird city at close quarters.

Legend has it that St Bees takes its name from an Irish nun, St Bega, who founded a small nunnery here in the seventh century, after escaping from Ireland when a forced marriage to a Norse chieftain was planned. The land, on a three-mile stretch around the headland, was granted to her by Lord Egremont after he told her, in midsummer, that she could have as much land as was covered by snow. The next day it snowed and she was granted the land.

From the car park at St Bees take the cliff-top path. The paths are steep in places and being a natural site they are unimproved and have several stiles. Follow the path along the south head before dipping down to Fleswick Bay between the two headlands.

❶ The seabird inhabitants of the south head are mainly herring gulls, fulmar and razorbill. The north head has much greater diversity and numbers. The small marshy area at the start of the cliffs holds breeding sedge warblers. Rock pipits occur right from the start but can be difficult to spot as they flit among the rocks. Best views are usually obtained at Fleswick Bay where they often forage on the tide line. Wheatears favour the turf and boulder walls. The gorse-dominated areas, especially the large area close to Fleswick Bay, allow excellent views of stonechat, whitethroat and linnet. The wonderfully carmine red breast and forehead of the latter never fails to impress those seeing it for the first time. Little owls have also been seen in the same area, often sitting on a post usually towards dusk.

From the top of the headland it is well worth scanning the sea, for besides the breeding seabirds gannets are regular passing to and fro from their breeding colony on Scar rocks off the Galloway coast. With favourable onshore winds Manx shearwaters, and occasionally petrels and skuas, can be seen. Terns are also regular, especially in spring and late summer.

For much of the growing season the cliffs and footpath edges are alive with colour, with drifts of thrift, sea campion and scurvy grass vying with the gorse for attention. Butterflies to look out for include gatekeeper, grayling and small copper.

From Fleswick Bay follow the coastal path onto the north headland stopping at each of the three observation platforms. It is often worthwhile going a short distance past the third observation platform then returning by the same route back to St Bees car park.

❶ To many bird watchers the highlight of a trip to St Bees is the sight of a black guillemot, for the head is the only regular breeding site in England for this attractive species. They favour the boulder-strewn beach of Fleswick Bay. This is the rarest of St Bees breeding seabirds with only around five pairs nesting, so finding one can take some time. Searching through the rafts of auks floating on the water is usually successful as the dazzling white wing patches and crimson legs contrasting with the black plumage really makes it stand out. Puffins are also rare breeders here, with perhaps 10–15 pairs. This scarcity is due to the fact that there is little suitable breeding habitat at St Bees but they can be spotted either on the cliffs or on the sea from the observation platforms, with the most northerly platform usually the most reliable. With patience you will be rewarded with good views of this delightful seabird with its wonderful multi-coloured bill, at its best

Tawny owl

Mike Malpass

The tawny owl is the commonest owl in Lakeland. It is very much a woodland owl although it does occur in well-timbered farmland. During day time it can be difficult to see, for it spends the daylight hours sitting bolt upright in a tree hollow or on a branch close to the tree trunk. However, a visit after dark will quickly reveal its presence, for the bird is very vocal, especially in spring and later in the year when the young have left the nest. The call of the male is the well-known loud hoot to which the female responds with the 'ke-wick ke-wick' call. Very occasionally they can be heard calling during the day. The young stay with their parents until early winter, during which period they learn to hunt for themselves and become increasingly vocal.

Although searching suitable sites can often locate day-time roosting owls, probably the best way is to investigate any marked commotion of anxious alarm notes. If they locate a roosting owl many smaller species will join in scalding the bird, and if it persists the owl will often seek a new hiding place.

The prey is predominately small mammals, especially wood mice and voles, although it will also take small birds up to the size of a blackbird and young rabbits or even large insects. It relies on its acute hearing to locate its prey, while its soft plumage allows a silent approach.

A late-evening visit from February through to October to any woodland of reasonable size on any of the walks should be rewarded with a bout of calling.

Walks: all walks except **18, 24, 25**

Barn owl

Very much a bird of the night, the best chances of seeing a barn owl are at dusk, silently quartering a field or caught briefly in car headlights. However on occasions, such as when feeding young or during a cold spell and food is short, it will hunt in broad daylight. Very much a bird of the lower reaches of valleys and the coastal plain, it needs suitable buildings in which to nest, although they will nest in large tree holes or in holes in disused quarries. The provision of nest boxes in buildings in both north and south Cumbria has been rewarded with an increase in breeding pairs. Also important is the presence of sufficient rough grassland harbouring a small mammal population which it can hunt.

Walks: **14, 21, 22, 23, 24**

Mike Malpass

Mike Malpass

Goosander

This attractive duck is a feature of the area's river systems and lakes. A hole-nesting, diving duck it is a member of the saw bills group of wildfowl (so called because of the saw-toothed edges to the bill, designed to catch fish). Very much a freshwater bird, it has increased rapidly over the past fifty years. They are often seen in small groups flying along a river system. In late spring and early summer the females can be seen leading a flotilla of young birds along a stream or river. In winter the birds resort to the lakes, with Grasmere Bassenthwaite and Derwentwater being favoured sites.

Walks: 1, 2, 3, 4, 5, 6, 7, 10, 11, 12, 13, 15, 16, 17, 19, 20, 21, 23, 24, 25, 26, 27, 29

Mike Malpass

Mike Malpass

Goldeneye

This winter visitor is quite widely distributed on lakes and tarns throughout Lakeland and along the coast from September to mid April. Largest numbers occur on Windermere, Bassenthwaite and Derwentwater. Usually occurs either singly or in small groups on most waters. Inland sightings are mainly of females or immatures (as illustrated) but adult males occur frequently on the coast and inland in spring.

Walks: **1, 2, 3, 4, 5, 6, 7, 10, 11, 12, 13, 15, 16, 17, 19, 20, 21, 23, 24, 25, 26, 27, 29**

Great crested grebe

With so many water areas within Lakeland one would perhaps expect great crested grebes to be a common breeding bird. However this is a species that prefers relatively shallow water with ample vegetation in which to conceal its nest. Most of the lakes lack these two major requirements, with only Bassenthwaite, Esthwaite, Grasmere and Derwentwater of the major lakes providing suitable habitat. The largest number of breeding pairs occurs at Hodbarrow, where around fifteen pairs nest almost colonially. Outside the breeding season the bird is widely spread and can occur on almost any lake or tarn, and numbers resort to the sea.

Walks: **1, 2, 3, 4, 10, 12, 15, 16, 17, 20, 21, 23, 24, 25, 26, 27**

Mike Malpass

Grey heron

A heron in patient statuesque pose in the shallow waters of a tarn or river is a familiar sight. For breeding it tends to be a bird of river systems, with marked concentrations in the Derwent and Kent valleys, where it nests colonially in traditional woodland sites. In total there are up to 300 pairs in Cumbria spread between around thirty heronries. After breeding it spreads across the countryside and can be seen, often singularly, on any stretch of open water, including the estuaries.

All *walks*

Mike Malpass

Peter Smith

Little egret

This small, all-white heron with black legs and yellow feet, is at the time of writing, a regular visitor in increasing numbers to the Morecambe Bay coast, mainly from mid summer to late winter; at peak up to forty have occurred at South Walney. Smaller numbers also occur irregularly on the West Cumbrian and Solway coasts, but it is very rare inland. It must be viewed as a potential colonist for it first bred in Britain in Dorset as recently as 1995 and in the period since then it has spread and now breeds as far north as Cheshire. It would be a very welcome addition to Cumbrian breeding birds.

Walks: 15, 16, 17, 18, 19, 20, 21, 23, 24, 25, 26

Arctic skua (*opposite*)

A bird of passage passing in small numbers along the coast and very rarely inland. Occurs mainly in May and August to September while migrating to and from its Arctic breeding grounds. Has two colour phases (light and dark). In flight it is rather gull-like but appears much darker and is strikingly fast, despite its rather relaxed wing beat. It pursues gulls and terns to force them to disgorge fish, displaying superior speed and aerobatics.

Walks: 15, 16, 17, 20, 21, 23, 24, 25

Mike Malpass

Kittiwake

The kittiwake is a remarkably gentle and attractive-looking gull of grey and white plumage, with pale yellow bill and distinctive black legs and wing tips. Immature kittiwakes, or tarrochs, have a black band at the base of the tail and neck and a distinctive diagonal black band across the wings.

    The red sandstone cliffs of St Bees Head provide the only suitable nest site in Cumbria for this attractive gull. Recent counts suggest a population of c. 1200 pairs, and nearly all are concentrated on the north head of the RSPB reserve. During courtship, nest building and incubation the colony rings with pleasant calls of 'kitti-waake, kitti-waake', with an ascending emphasis on the last syllable, so it is easy to see where the bird gets its name from. They build their nests often close together on narrow rather insecure looking ledges on the steepest part of the cliff. The nest is a collection of seaweed and grass held together by mud and clay.

    Kittiwakes are common passage migrants and winter visitors along the west Cumbria coast but usually only occur in numbers within the more sheltered waters of Morecambe Bay and the Solway during periods of westerly gales.

Walks: 15, 16, 17, 18, 20, 21, 23, 24, 25

Sandwich tern (*opposite*)

This largest of our breeding terns is quite easy to recognise with its heavier build and short-forked tail separating it at once from the other slender, long-streamered terns. A regular early spring and autumn passage migrant along the coast, its only breeding site in Cumbria is the RSPB reserve of Hodbarrow on the Duddon estuary. Here in recent years up to 350 pairs have nested annually, usually on the specially prepared island close to the bird watching hide, a site they share with little terns and many black-headed gulls. One of our earliest migrants, the first birds can arrive in early to mid March and usually get down to nesting activities soon after arriving.

Walks: 15, 16, 17, 18, 19, 20, 21, 23, 24, 25

Mike Malpass

Black-headed Gull

Any water's edge where humans regularly congregate will have its attendant flock of black-headed gulls touting for food scraps. Its breeding colonies vary in size and can change rapidly from year to year. The major ones are either on nature reserves such as Hodbarrow or on islands in lakes or reservoirs such as Killington. Birds can travel some distance from their colonies in search of food and are often seen in small flocks on upland pastures. Numbers increase in winter as birds from northern Europe arrive to escape the severe winter weather. Large numbers gather to roost on the sand flats of the estuaries and on a few inland waters, often flying some distances from their inland feeding areas and mixing with the other numerous inland gull in winter, the common gull.

All walks

Mike Malpass

Peter Smith

Puffin

With its multi-coloured beak crammed with fish and standing upright on a sea cliff, the puffin is every new birdwatchers must-see on a visit to the coast. In Cumbria puffins are restricted to the red sandstone cliffs of St Bees Head. Here in recent years the population has been put at 10–15 pairs, all on the north head of this imposing cliff. The RSPB have provided three viewing platforms and the most northern one gives the best chance of seeing this bird in its characteristic pose. Birds can also be located by searching through the large flocks of auks which swim offshore, where their colourful bills and red legs stand out.

Puffins are usually present at St Bees from March to early August but the best time to see them is May and June. Outside the breeding season the birds disperse to the open seas and are only rarely seen offshore.

Walk: 18

Lapwing (*opposite*)

This attractive wader with its bizarre tall crest, rounded wings, glossy green back and rich chestnut patches above and below the tail, is easily identified. It is still fairly widely distributed as a breeding bird. During the Atlas survey of 1997 to 2001 the Cumbria population was estimated at 23,000 pairs. Its strongholds are the Solway basin, the Eden Valley and the North Pennines, and the coastal areas of West Cumbria and the edges of Morecambe Bay. It is almost completely absent from the valleys and moors of central Lakeland. In former years it was much commoner but agricultural intensification has brought about a serious decline in many areas, especially where silage cutting is undertaken. It is also a passage migrant and an abundant winter visitor to the mudflats, coastal grassland and estuaries of Morecambe Bay and the Solway.

Arriving on the breeding grounds during the first mild spell of late winter, the males establish their territories with erratic aerial dances accompanied by excited bouts of calling. The male attracts the female by scraping a hollow in frenzied haste and bending forward with his breast to the ground while displaying his rich chestnut tail patches to entrance the female. Both sexes share incubation and care of the young. Flocking starts in late June and most have left the breeding grounds by early July to congregate in large flocks in lowland areas adjacent to the coastline. Numbers are supplemented during the autumn and winter, particularly during periods of hard frost. Ringing has shown that many of these migrants originate from Scandinavian countries.

Walks: 10, 12, 13, 14, 15, 16, 17, 19, 20, 21, 23, 27

Fulmar

The sight of a fulmar gracefully and effortlessly soaring along a cliff top is a wonderful experience. Exploiting the air currents alongside the cliff face, it patrols on straight wings forwards and backwards. The main colony of c. 60 pairs is on the red stone headland of St Bees where it nests on both the north and south heads. A small colony of c. 12 pairs has been established recently a little further north on the cliffs between Whitehaven and Parton. Fulmars visit the cliffs as early as

Mike Malpass

December and the last birds don't leave until early September. There are marked spring and autumn movements along the coast, many of which are probably immature birds for Fulmars do not breed until they are at least seven years old. Sightings in mid winter are few for this is a truly oceanic bird wandering well out into the Atlantic and even crossing it, as ringing recoveries along the Canadian coast show.

Walks: 15, 16, 17, 18, 20, 21, 23, 24, 25

Mike Malpass

Mike Malpass

Snipe

A snipe 'drumming', once a common sound over damp pastures and bogs, is heard much less frequently today. The drainage of hill pastures and the general intensification of agriculture has produced serious declines both in overall numbers and in breeding and wintering birds. Today its major haunts are the eastern fells rising from both the Lune and Eden valleys and the fells around Shap. It also occurs as a breeding bird on the low land around Bassenthwaite and Derwentwater. In winter it can usually be found nowadays in any marshy area. When flushed it rises steeply with a quick zigzag flight and gives a rather harsh call.

Walks: 3, 4 10, 12, 13, 14, 15, 16, 17, 19, 21, 23, 24, 25, 26, 27, 28

Mike Malpass

Curlew

The curlew's long, de-curved bill and large size, along with its distinctive call, makes this species one of our best-known waders. It is a summer visitor to much of Lakeland, very often the first sign of spring on the fells, and an abundant winter resident passage migrant along the coast. For nesting, curlews need damp soil and a wide vista so they nest on a range of open habitats from moorland to lowland meadows and pastures. It is most abundant on the moors and upland pastures in eastern and southern Cumbria but is largely absent from the central steeper uplands.

Walks: **3, 12, 13, 14, 15, 16, 17, 19, 20, 21, 23, 24, 25, 26, 27, 28**

Common sandpiper (*opposite*)

A summer visitor to many Lakeland rivers, streams, lakes and tarns, the common sandpiper has a characteristically crouched posture with a continuously bobbing of the rear body. It skims over the water with shallow quivering wing beats giving a repeated trilling call.
The first birds usually arrive at their breeding haunts in early April, with the breeding cycle extending over a period of about ten weeks. With the completion of breeding there is a gradual drift to the coast and most birds have migrated by mid September.

Walks: **1, 2, 3, 4, 6, 7, 10, 11, 12, 13, 14, 15, 16, 17, 19, 20, 21, 23, 24, 27, 29**

Peter Smith

Golden Eagle

Whether soaring on its two-metre plus wing span or perched on a crag or rock, the golden eagle is truly a majestic bird. A pair nested in the Riggindale valley near Haweswater for thirty two years from 1969, rearing sixteen young during this period. At the time of writing, sadly only a single male is resident in the area. There seems little hope of a female joining him for the population in south-west Scotland – from where the original pair almost certainly came – is also in decline. Buzzards are often mistaken for eagles but in flight the golden eagle dwarfs the buzzard, being almost twice as large in wing span with large broad wings, 'fingered' wing tips, and a powerful bill. The power of the bird shows in its flight, with typically a few wing beats followed by a long glide as it heads toward its perch on a rock or tree.

Walk: 4

Mike Malpass

Mike Malpass

Osprey

Formerly a rather scarce passage migrant to its Scottish breeding haunts, the successful nesting in 2000 of the first pair of ospreys to breed in Lakeland for at least 170 years was greeted with great joy by Cumbria's bird watchers. Since then the population has increased to at least three pairs, one of which nested on specially erected nesting platforms within the Forestry Commission's Dodd Wood on the side of Bassenthwaite, which opened for viewing in 2001. From excellent viewpoints visitors can watch the nesting activities of these superb birds, and from various observation sites it is also possible to watch them fishing in Bassenthwaite Lake. This spectacular sight starts when the bird hovers well above the lake before plunging feet first into the water in a plume of spray, to emerge with a firmly grasped fish in its talons. It will then either fly back to the nest or eat the fish itself, perched on a dead tree or log. Live pictures of the osprey's activities at Dodd Wood are beamed to the Visitor Centre at Whinlatter Forest Park and shown on a giant video wall.

With the increasing population both within Lakeland and in Scotland, ospreys have become regular passage migrants at several other lakes and rivers. The breeding adults pass quickly but immature birds often stay at such sites for several weeks, raising hopes that this superbly majestic bird will further extend its breeding range within Cumbria and further afield. During spring and autumn migration it may be seen as a 'fly over' on all the walks but most especially nine and ten (Bassenthwaite)

All walks but particularly 9 and 10

Buzzard (*opposite*)

With its distinctive mewing call and its habit of soaring on broad-fingered wings, the buzzard is a familiar sight throughout Lakeland and is now our commonest bird of prey. It is an adaptable species occurring across a wide range of habitats and taking a large variety of prey. Much of the population nests in trees, but on the treeless fells it resorts to ledges on cliffs. Buzzards spend much of their day perched on some concealed vantage point watching for unsuspecting prey, of which rabbits are perhaps the most favoured.

All walks

Mike Malpass

Peregrine

This spectacular raptor is the bird of the Lakeland mountains and fells. It nests widely throughout upland Lakeland and in recent years, by readily taking to quarries and even slag banks, it has extended its range to many lowland areas. Peregrine enthusiasts claim that the 125 or more breeding pairs within Cumbria represents the highest density of nesting peregrines anywhere in the world. The Lakeland population is closely monitored and protected by a band of dedicated enthusiasts. The more exposed eyries are temporarily deserted in winter, with birds heading for the coast where they find easy pickings among the flocks of wintering waders. Lowland pairs remain close to their breeding haunts, often perching on their chosen nest cliff and objecting strongly to any intrusion.

All walks

Cuckoo (*opposite*)

The instantly recognisable call of the male cuckoo is known by birdwatchers and non-bird watchers alike as a harbinger of spring. The bubbling call of the female is, however, less well known. Birds are first heard in late April and the male delivers his far-carrying call from an elevated perch. The infamous lifestyle of the cuckoo is well known and in Lakeland its main host is certainly the meadow pipit. The female closely watches the activities of her potential foster birds, darting in quickly to lay her egg and remove one of her host's when the opportunity arises. Many habitats are occupied but in recent years there has been a marked contraction of both range and numbers. This has been linked to the decline in its main prey, the hairy caterpillar. At present in many areas they appear to have withdrawn to the moorland edge and many former territories in other habitats have become vacant.

Walks: 1, 2, 3, 4, 5, 6, 8, 11, 14, 16, 20, 21, 22, 27, 30

Kestrel

This adaptable raptor is instantly recognisable by its well-known hovering action. Several other raptors hover briefly but none have perfected the art as well as the kestrel. Well distributed throughout Lakeland, it occurs in the more open habitats, including fellside and farmland, as long as there is sufficient cover for its main prey, voles. However, it takes a wide range of prey, including many invertebrates, especially in late summer when numbers will venture onto the higher fells to catch the emerging larger insects. In winter it tends to gravitate to lower ground, including the coastal strip.

All walks

Mike Malpass

Mike Malpass

Mike Malpass

Jay

A raucous call and the flash of a white rump are usually the first indications that this wonderfully brightly coloured but secretive member of the crow family is about. Very much

Mike Malpass

a woodland bird, it occurs in all types of woodland, including coniferous plantations and well-timbered hillsides or farmland. However, the largest numbers occur in the deciduous woodlands of south Lakeland. Food is regularly collected from the woodland floor and at times well outside the woodland edge, In winter it feeds principally on acorns, large numbers of which it collects and buries, resulting in new oak trees from those which are not retrieved.

Walks: **1, 2, 3, 5, 6, 7, 8, 9, 10, 13, 14 19, 21, 27, 28, 30**

Dipper (*opposite*)

No bird-watching visit to Lakeland is complete without good views of that dapper resident of fast-flowing streams, the dipper. Best views are obtained when it perches on a rock around which the water swirls and tumbles, its white breast prominent; with its short tail uplifted it bobs spasmodically before plunging into the water with a small splash. In shallow water it walks to locate its prey but in deeper water it dives under the water and swims with its wings, its course beneath the surface often revealed by a line of rising bubbles.

It is well distributed throughout central Lakeland but is at its commonest on the tributaries of the Eden and Lune. The Atlas survey suggested a total population of perhaps 3000 pairs in the whole of Cumbria. It is resident throughout the year, only leaving during the now very infrequent severe cold spells that freeze all the streams. The birds are very territorial, defending their chosen length of stream with song and chase. They regularly sing in winter, although the main season for song is from December through to May.

Dippers build their domed nest close to water, favoured sites being under bridges or over-hanging banks or even behind waterfalls. They are early nesters, with the first brood of youngsters often on the wing by late March. They can easily be identified for they lack the chestnut band of the adults.

Walks: 1, 2, 3, 4, 5, 6, 7, 10, 11, 12, 13, 14, 19, 27, 29

Kingfisher

With so many water areas one might have expected kingfishers to be quite common in Lakeland. However, for breeding this bird needs soft, usually sandy, banks in which to excavate its nesting hole, a habitat that is missing from much of Lakeland. So its breeding distribution is quite limited, being mainly in the valleys of the Eden, Kent and Derwent. Outside the breeding season it is more widely distributed, although it prefers to fish in shallow water, usually with over-hanging branches, so tarns, rivers and streams are its preferred habitats. Late summer is probably the best time to look for this highly colourful bird, as family groups start to disperse and they can turn up on any watercourse, including salt marshes.

Walks: 1, 2, 3, 7, 10, 12, 13, 15, 16, 17, 21, 23, 24, 25, 26, 27, 29

Mike Malpass

Coal tit

The diminutive coal tit is easily identified by a white patch running up the nape and bisecting the black cap, while the black bib contrasts with prominent white cheeks. Young birds, however, are tinged with yellow. The call is a thin 'zee', while the song is a repetitious 'cher-tee cher-tee', usually delivered from the top of a conifer.

This is the tit of coniferous woodland. It gets over the lack of natural nest holes in planted conifers by using holes low down, often in the ground, under rocks or in a tree bole. Because of

Mike Malpass

this ability it is often the only tit species nesting in commercial conifer plantations. With the extension and maturing of such plantations throughout much of Lakeland it has increased markedly in recent years, helped as well by the long run of mild winters. Post-breeding dispersal can lead to a marked irrupting out of the forests during the autumn, leading to many sightings well away from the breeding haunts, with large numbers coming to garden feeders. Here the habit of caching food can be watched as birds fly off with seeds to hide in a hole or crevice. Studies have shown that they regularly relocate such hidden caches.

All walks except 18 and 25

Siskin (*opposite*)

Although the siskin is a comparatively recent colonist of Lakeland, it has increased massively in recent years. It is very much a bird of mature conifer plantations, including the widely planted sitka spruce; as these have spread and matured the population has responded. The largest breeding populations are to be found in the Forestry Commission's extensive forests at Grizedale and Whinlatter. Here they feed on the seed from the spruce and pine cones.

This delightful little finch is also a regular winter visitor and passage migrant. When the pine cones become exhausted or fail they frequent stands of birch and riverside alders. They often mix with redpolls and goldfinches, where its greenish plumage and short-forked tail, as well as the black head of the male, distinguish it from its companions. They will regularly visit the same group of trees for several weeks, where this acrobatic little finch often hangs upside down to pick out the alder and birch seeds.

In some areas late winter natural food appears to be running out and the siskin moves in numbers to gardens, where it will happily take peanuts and a wide range of seeds.

Walks: 1, 2, 4, 5, 6, 7, 8, 9, 10, 11, 12, 13, 14, 17, 19, 21, 22, 23, 27, 28, 29

Goldcrest

This delightful gem, adorned with a broad yellow crown stripe, is our smallest bird. It is usually located by its high-pitched call and song as it actively flits from branch to branch in search of small invertebrates. Mainly, but not exclusively, a bird of conifer woodland, it is widely distributed throughout Lakeland wherever there is woodland. Highest densities occur in the larger coniferous forests and certainly the afforestation of the uplands in many areas has benefited this bird. In

Mike Malpass

winter some move out into hedgerows and gardens, often attached to tit flocks. Ringing has shown that some of our wintering birds come all the way from Scandinavia, an amazing feat for a bird that weighs only 5–6 grams.

All walks except 25

Mike Malpass

Yellowhammer

Well known for his popular song, 'a little bit of bread and no cheese', the male yellowhammer, resplendent in his canary-yellow plumage, delivers his ditty from February through to mid August from the top of a bush or hedgerow. During the breeding season it frequents scrubby hillsides and open mixed farmland with small fields and hedgerows. Although still widely distributed, especially in the Solway plain, parts of the Eden Valley and western Lakeland, it has declined recently in many areas, a decline that

Mike Malpass

appears to be linked to agricultural intensification. In winter it will come to gardens but only if seed is provided on the ground.

Walks: 1, 2, 3, 5, 11, 14, 18, 21, 22, 30

Nuthatch

Now widely distributed and common throughout Lakeland, nuthatches have increased dramatically over the past few decades. In an Atlas survey in the early 1970s it was found in only eight localities but twenty years later it had spread throughout Lakeland wherever there were trees, and it is now abundant in many Lakeland valleys. The loud ringing call and song make it easy to locate. When feeding it runs both up and down trunks searching for insects or nuts; it fixes the latter firmly in cracks in the bark and hammers until it extracts the

Mike Malpass

kernel. It also plasters mud around its chosen nest hole to make it a suitable size. It will also nest in nest boxes, where it also plasters mud both around the hole and inside the lid. In winter it is a regular visitor to garden feeding stations.

Walks: 1, 2, 3, 5, 6, 7, 8, 9, 10, 11, 13, 19, 26, 27

Redstart

When seen clearly the male redstart is a joy to behold, its red breast contrasting with the black throat and white forehead. However, in the dappled light of its preferred habitat – mature deciduous woodland – patience is needed to be rewarded with a good view. The male usually sings perched high up in the trees. Both sexes constantly flick their orange-red tails, from which they get their name.

Redstarts are well distributed throughout the valleys of central Lakeland. It is also to be found in the mature valley oak woods and in farmland with scattered

Mike Malpass

mature trees and overgrown hedges. It nests in tree holes but is not averse to holes in stone walls or even buildings. This summer migrant usually arrives in late April and the male sings his short, sweet song on arrival to establish his territory. After the young have fledged they can often be seen in family groups along hedgerows far from mature woodland.

Walks: 1, 2, 3, 4, 5, 6, 7, 8, 9, 10, 11, 13, 14, 15, 16, 19, 21, 24, 27, 28, 29, 30

Bullfinch

A plaintive whistle and the flash of a white rump as the bird heads for cover is usually the first clue that bullfinches are present. With patience good views can be obtained of the wonderfully colourful male and his rather dowdy partner. Rather local in its distribution, it needs extensive patches of woodland understorey or thick hedgerows to prosper. These are found most commonly in the southern valleys and in scattered pockets in most other

Lakeland valleys, but are absent from many mature valley woodlands. Resident throughout the year, it is seen at its best in spring as it feasts on the opening buds of trees and bushes. Recently it has taken to visiting garden feeders, a habit which may aid winter survival.

Walks: 1, 2, 3, 5, 8, 10, 11, 12, 13, 14, 27, 28, 29, 30

Mike Malpass

Spotted flycatcher

Many birds catch flying insects but none so expertly as the spotted flycatcher. It perches on a post or dead branch that overlooks an open area and when an insect is spotted it sallies out, following each turn of its prey before making a smart final catch, often with an audible click of the bill. It is the last of our summer visitors to arrive and frequents woodland, often found at the edge, in clearings, or in large gardens. Although well distributed throughout the Lakeland valleys it has, along with several trans-Saharan migrants, declined in recent years.

Walks 1, 2, 3, 5, 6, 7, 8, 9, 10, 11, 12, 13, 14, 15, 16, 19, 21, 22, 27, 28, 29, 30

Mike Malpass

Mike Malpass

Pied flycatcher

The pied flycatcher is one of the special birds of the native, mainly oak woodlands of almost all Lakeland valleys. Often abundant, it arrives in late April and for the next two to three weeks it is easy to see as the male (above), which arrives first, sings from a dead branch and regularly visits suitable nest holes to attract a female (below). They are also quite visible when feeding young but as soon as the young fledge they disappear into the tree canopy. They readily take to nest boxes and several schemes operate within Lakeland.

Listen for the sweet, simple song which is regularly repeated, especially early in the season. The male's trim black-and-white plumage makes it easy to pick out but the much duller female, with a white patch on the wings, is often harder to locate.

Walks: 1, 2, 3, 4, 5, 6, 7, 9, 10, 11, 13, 14, 15, 19, 27, 28, 29

Mike Malpass

Mike Malpass

Tree pipit (*opposite*)

Despite its rather sombre plumage the tree pipit is an easy bird to locate, for its exuberant song and characteristic song flight set it apart. The song is delivered from a tree top from which it launches itself upward, singing all the time, then parachutes down again, very often but not always to the same tree.

Widely distributed throughout much of central Lakeland it prefers open woodland and hillsides with scattered trees. Recently cleared but regenerating coniferous forests are also occupied. The first birds arrive in late April but May and the first half of June are the best time to locate this splendid songster.

Walks: 1, 2, 3, 4, 5, 6, 7, 8, 9, 10, 11, 13, 14, 15, 19, 27, 28, 30

Male

Stan Craig

Whinchat

This summer visitor prefers upland areas where there is a good mixture of bracken, gorse, heather and open grassland. It is has declined recently in many areas and is now quite a difficult bird to locate. The Furness fells and the northern Pennines have the highest densities. When present it is an easy bird to locate due to the typical chat habit of perching on bushes or fence posts flicking its tail.

It often occupies the same areas as stonechat, from which it can be distinguished by its prominent white stripe above the eye and its streaked head and back. Where they occur together stonechats tend to dominate whinchats, being slightly larger and more robust. The increase in the stonechat population may be one reason for the whinchat's decline, although habitat degradation in its wintering areas in sub-Saharan Africa may also be to blame.

Walks: 2, 3, 4, 14, 15, 21, 22

Mike Malpass

Female

Male

Mike Malpass

Stonechat

The male stonechat is a conspicuous bird with black head, white collar and shoulder patch contrasting with a rich chestnut breast. He flaunts his bright colours from the top of a bush or fence post and the duller female is often close by.

The recent rapid increase and spread of the stonechat within Lakeland is probably due a succession of mild winters. Rough open country with a thick ground cover of gorse, heather, bracken or rank grass is the ideal habitat. It is more generally distributed in western Lakeland than the east. In recent winters numbers have remained in the uplands but others move to the coast where they are joined by the upland wintering birds during a cold spell. In winter birds are usually in pairs and are easy to locate because of their habit of perching conspicuously.

Walks: 1, 2, 3, 4, 6, 11, 14, 15, 16, 17, 18, 20, 21, 22, 23, 24, 27, 30

Mike Malpass

Female

Whitethroat

With its habit of singing from a prominent perch, from which it often indulges in a short, bouncy song-flight, the whitethroat is one of the easiest warblers to locate. The conspicuous white throat and rusty brown wings are distinctive. The first birds arrive in mid to late April, song and territory establishment gets underway on arrival, with a peak of activity in early May. The preferred habitat is low scrub, especially bramble tangles and overgrown hedgerows with plenty of thick cover in which to conceal its nest. It is at its most abundant in the coastal and lowland areas of Cumbria with only small numbers penetrating the central and eastern valleys.

Mike Malpass

Walks: 2, 3, 5, 8, 12, 13, 15, 17 18, 20, 21, 23, 24, 26

Sedge warbler

This summer visitor is mainly restricted to areas of wet vegetation. It is common around the developing fen areas of Siddick Pond, Bassenthwaite and Derwenwater and also occurs widely in isolated pockets of fen or pond edge especially on the Solway plain and along the coastal strip. Its hurried, spirited song is often given from the reed tops or from a bush and often develops into an almost vertical song flight. By mid April the first males have arrived and they sing incessantly to attract a mate, but once mated they sing much less. Return migration starts in early August and most are gone by mid September.

Walks: 2, 3, 12, 13, 15, 17, 18, 20, 21, 23, 24

Mike Malpass

Treecreeper

This species is so aptly named, an avian
mouse which runs up a tree! The stiff tail
lends support as it progresses furtively up a
trunk starting at the bottom. It often climbs
in a spiral, to reach the smaller branches,
where it tends to traverse upside down as it
searches promising cracks for hidden insects
or larvae. Then, with a quick drooping flight,
it descends to the next tree. Its delicately
variegated colours blend in very well with
its trunk and branch habitat, although its
silvery white breast often catches the eye.
Its large feet are well adapted to its lifestyle.

Well distributed in all our deciduous
woodlands, it only occasionally visits conifer
plantations. The nest is built in a crevice,
and can be behind a section of loose bark,
in a large crack or behind ivy on the trunk of
a tree, and it will take to specially designed
nest boxes which imitate its crevice
requirements.

Walks: 1, 2, 3, 5, 6, 7, 8, 10, 11, 12, 13, 14,
19, 28, 29, 30

Stan Craig

Grey wagtail

The grey wagtail is a characteristic bird of fast-flowing streams so it is well distributed
throughout Lakeland, often sharing the same stretch of river or stream with dippers. Both
species also share the habit of perching on exposed stones from which the more colourful
grey wagtail launches a quick darting turn to catch a passing insect. It is not, however,
restricted entirely to upland water courses, as it also breeds on fast-flowing sections of
lowland rivers and on man-made features such as weirs and mill races. In winter it can often
be found away from rivers on flooded fields or even around farm buildings.

All walks except 18, 28

Mike Malpass

Meadow pipit

The meadow pipit is the most abundant breeding bird of the Lakeland fells, and its rather thin, trilling song is a constant companion on any fell walk in spring. The song flight starts on the ground, rises sharply on fluttering wings, then parachutes back to the ground.

In both early spring and autumn it is an abundant passage migrant both inland and on the coast as birds head to and from the breeding and wintering areas. Ringing has shown that many of our breeding birds winter in France and Iberia.

Mike Malpass

All walks except 5, 7, 8 and 9

Crossbill

The crossbill is the iconic bird of conifer forest, taking its name from its most striking and distinctive character, its crossed mandible tips, an adaptation that allows it to open the spruce, larch and pine cones with ease. The first sign of their presence is usually the distinctive 'chip chip' flight call. Flocks feed silently in the tree tops, their movements parrot-like as they clamber along the branches, often walking sideways and reaching down to wrench off a cone. Confined to breeding mainly in the extensive pine forests of Whinlatter, Grizedale and Crummock, numbers vary from year to year. Larger numbers breed after an irruption in the previous year. These arrivals, which occur every few years are caused by a failure of the cone crop within its main range in Europe. When an irruption is on flocks start to arrive in late summer and can turn up almost any where there are conifers.

Walks: 4, 5, 6, 8, 9, 10, 13, 28

Mike Malpass

Lesser redpoll

This active little finch is predominantly a bird of young and developing woodland. In Lakeland it is thinly and erratically distributed and breeds in birch and willow scrub and also in young conifer plantations, but declines rapidly as the trees mature, so populations can be quite transitory. Where conditions are suitable it

Mike Malpass

can be quite common, often nesting in a rather loose colony, although some pairs will nest in isolation. It is a very active and rather erratic flier, 'dancing' in flight and delivering its rather simple song. There is often a very marked passage in early May, suggesting that many of our breeding birds winter further south, a theory supported by some ringing recoveries

Outside the breeding season it forms flocks with siskins and goldfinches and often resorts to stands of birch and riverside alders. It is a very acrobatic feeder, often hanging upside down from the swaying branches to reach the seeds. At such times they can be quite approachable, especially when they drop to the ground in search of fallen seeds.

Walks: 1, 2, 3, 4, 5, 6, 7, 8, 9, 10, 12, 13, 14, 17, 23, 27, 29

Swallow

This much-loved summer visitor is widely distributed within Lakeland, wherever there are buildings suitable for nesting or open country to feed over. In late summer it assembles in flocks prior to migration and roosts in reed beds such as those on Bassenthwaite and Siddick Pond. In recent years it has also taken to roosting in maize fields.

All walks

Mike Malpass

Raven (*opposite*)

This majestic bird is easily told from other more common crows by its heavy bill and neck, large size and wedge-shaped tail. It also has a quite measured but powerful flight and a wonderful deep, croaking call. Widely distributed throughout central Lakeland it nests mainly on cliffs, including the sea cliffs of St Bees Head. Recently the population has increased and spread and several pairs are now nesting in trees, allowing colonisation of new and potentially more productive habitats. Ravens are early nesters, often starting in late February. After fledging they will stay together as a family throughout the summer. They also roost communally at times in winter, a wonderful sight and sound as they retire to a cliff or group of trees for the night.

All walks

Mike Malpass

Great spotted woodpecker

A well-distributed resident of Lakeland's woodlands – the black and white plumage with a dash of red and its bizarre 'drumming' habit make this a popular bird. The drumming is its territorial 'song' but it is of course one of the few territorial calls which is not produced vocally. To watch a bird drumming against a tree trunk is one of the highlights of spring. Mature woodland is the main habitat in Lakeland but it also occurs in smaller numbers in conifer plantations and gardens. Standing dead wood is important both for feeding and for nest holes, and dead or dying silver birches are often chosen for the latter. Birds regularly visit garden feeders at all times of the year, some pairs even bringing their recently fledged young to take advantage of the easy pickings.

All walks except **18, 26**

Peter Smith

Peter Smith

Green woodpecker

Despite its bright, almost exotic, colours this large woodpecker is often quite difficult to see. First clue to its presence is the distinctive loud laughing call or 'yaffle' which is heard throughout the year. It is well distributed in all the wooded river valleys in Lakeland with the strongest presence in the south of the area. This woodpecker prefers open deciduous woodland, well-timbered hillsides and farmland, and large gardens. It feeds a great deal on the ground in fields and fell side close to woodland wherever there is an abundance of ants, its favoured prey. Locating a feeding bird gives the best opportunity for a prolonged view so scanning areas of unimproved and timbered grassland is recommended.

Walks: 1, 2, 3, 5, 6, 7,8, 10, 11, 13, 14 19, 27, 28, 29, 30

Peter Smith

Red squirrel

The red squirrel is one of the most charming of Lakeland mammals, especially when seen sitting on its haunches with plume tail and tufted ears, characteristically holding a tasty morsel in its forepaws. Contrary to popular belief, red squirrels do not hibernate and occur throughout the seasons in Lakeland's deciduous and coniferous woodlands. The control of the invasive grey squirrel is a priority for the authorities and local conservationists, for it has spread alarmingly into the Lake District and southern Scotland. The greys are known to carry a poxvirus that causes few problems to themselves but is fatal to the reds. Once in a population of reds, squirrel poxvirus has devastating effects and can wipe out entire populations if not isolated. Research to address the plight of the diminishing red squirrel continues.

Walks: 2, 3, 4, 5, 6, 7, 8, 9, 10, 11, 13, 19, 27

Otter

The otter is making a comeback to the rivers, lakes and tarns of Lakeland and is by no means as rare as commonly imagined. Nevertheless any sighting of this fascinating mammal, usually during the quiet twilight hours, makes for a real red-letter day. During the daytime otters usually rest in their holt or lair, which is often a hole in the bank with the entrance under water. Their total length is about four feet, inclusive of the long thick tail that works efficiently as a rudder. Short powerful legs and completely webbed feet make it a most agile swimmer. Despite being superbly adapted for an aquatic life otters often travel across country at night seeking new feeding grounds, and their spraints, or droppings, provide evidence of their presence in particular localities.

Walks: 1, 3, 4, 7, 10, 12, 13, 17, 19

Peter Smith

when it returns to the cliff with its bill crammed with small fish giving it a bearded appearance

The most impressive spectacles at St Bees are the massed ranks of guillemots occupying every suitable ledge. The density on some ledges is such that birds incubating their single egg appear to huddle side by side, and those landing have to force a passage through the throng. The wonderful contrast of the sleek chocolate brown and white plumage against the red sandstone cliff, coupled with the constant movement and the cacophony of sound, is a wonderful experience. Recent counts suggest a population of 3000+ pairs. Its close relative the Razorbill nests in much smaller numbers with only about 125 pairs. With good views the two are easy to separate, with the razorbill's heavy bill with a white line that extends to the eye and the darker body being distinctive. Razorbills nest in a crevice typically under boulders and they often disappear quickly to the nest site after landing on the cliff.

Kittiwakes, that most oceanic of gulls, are St Bee's other abundant breeding bird with a recent estimate of 1200 pairs. Unlike the auks, kittiwakes build a nest on the cliffs so are never as concentrated as guillemots. The call from which the bird gets its name echoes in a chorus of 'kitti-wark, kitti-wark' from the nesting cliffs.

Cormorants nest in small numbers (30 pairs) and many of the nests are out of sight at the bottom of the cliff, but this large bird is easily picked out as they stand around in small groups on the rocks or fly along the cliffs.

The fulmar, a member of the petrel family, nests in small numbers (c. 50 pairs) scattered along the cliffs, where they prefer the larger more vegetated ledges. They are sheer joy to watch as they soar along the cliff edge with effortless elegance. Other nesting birds to watch out for include peregrine, kestrel and raven. Any sudden disturbance of the nesting seabirds usually betrays the presence of a hunting peregrine, however its main prey seems to be the many feral pigeons in the area.

The best time to visit the reserve is certainly from May to mid July. The first guillemots can return briefly to the cliffs around the turn of the year but numbers start to assemble at the colony in February, along with many of the other species. Early in the year they often appear nervous and flight out to sea if a person or boat appears. But as the season progress all species become strongly territorial. By mid July the young guillemots are ready to leave the ledges. They leave before they can fly, usually towards dusk, by jumping off the ledges with tiny wings flapping and their large feet spread out, often attended by an anxious adult. Once on the water their parents locate them by their loud incessant calling and escort them out to sea.

Discover Eskdale on the La'al Ratty

Redshank

Start: The approach here is fundamentally different from the preceding walks in that it offers an optional choice of travel by steam train on Lakeland's longest and oldest heritage line from Ravenglass to the heart of the Eskdale valley. The terminus railway station in Eskdale at Dalegarth, is the starting and finishing point of three recommended walks, selected for their varied habitat in the middle Eskdale valley, that may be done singly or as any permutation

Grid Ref: for Dalegarth Station NY175007

Time: Allow seven to eight hours for inclusive train journey and the three combined walks, taking care not to miss the last train back to Ravenglass

Grade: Easy

General: Refreshments, toilet and parking facilities at Ravenglass and Dalegarth stations. At least six trains operate per day on the Ravenglass and Eskdale (RER) steam railway, from mid March to November. A reduced winter service operates over Christmas and February half term. The RER station is adjacent to the main line railway station at Ravenglass and further details/timetables may be obtained by telephoning 01229717171 or from the website www.ravenglass-railway.co.uk

APPROPRIATELY, THREE OF THE much-admired veteran RER steam engines, resplendent in bright colours and in immaculate condition, are named after their namesake local rivers: Esk, Irt and Mite. Tourist lines such as the 'La'al Ratty' (so called because it was said to resemble a rat's tail!), as it is affectionately known, have become a feature of the landscape and have provided immense pleasure to countless hordes of people since the mid-Victorian era. Built to support the local iron ore industry, centred near the existing terminus at Boot, the RER originally opened on 20 November 1876.

Some of the birds that may be seen from the railway's slow-moving open carriages are described to provide a taster of the ornithological potential of Eskdale. Over the years the author has seen all of the species mentioned from the train, so keep your eyes open, though do not expect to see them all on the same day! Habitat diversity is the adopted theme and should be savoured from the train and while walking in the Eskdale valley. The term habitat as distinct from locality – alluding to geographical distribution – might be described as a type of environment in which a particular species likes to dwell and for which it is structurally adapted. The Lake District is rich in habitat diversity and the train ride itself embraces estuarine coastal marshes, tranquil woodlands, rocky crags, lowland pasture and gardens.

Before embarking on this journey of discovery it is well worth having a look at the historic village of Ravenglass, where the confluences of the rivers Esk, Irt and Mite form an estuary that flows between sand dunes into the Irish Sea. The northern shore at Drigg Point was once the largest black-headed gullery in Europe. There was also a thriving sandwich tern colony but since the late 1970s and 1980s it has been completely forsaken as a breeding colony by both species. On the south bank the sand dunes form part of an important botanical site that is the Eskmeal Dunes nature reserve. The footbridge alongside the railway viaduct over the River Mite is a good spot to observe the estuary at low tide, when waders and wildfowl gather to feed on the tidal mud flats.

After boarding the Ratty at Ravenglass several estuarine species may be seen along the tidal section of the Mite and the adjacent salt marsh. The post-war colonisation of red-breasted mergansers means they regularly occur along the tidal stretches of the three rivers and may be seen from the slow-moving train. The goosander prefers the upper freshwater reaches of the rivers and it is significant that the first confirmed breeding record in Cumbria occurred in 1950 on the River Esk. There are likely to be good views of cormorant and heron standing motionless in the shallow waters waiting for that tasty fish to pass by. Fidgety redshank, curlew, oystercatcher and occasional passage migrants such as the greenshank, seem to be constantly on the look out for danger and exercise their vocal prowess with strident warning calls. Flocks of greylag geese, shelduck and mallard, augmented

Santon Bridge

River Irt

to Holmrook

A595

Route of Ravenglass and Eskdale Railway

Ian's Wood

Muncaster Mill Bridge

River Esk

P

Muncaster Bridge

M

Ravenglass

Muncaster Castle

P

Walls Castle

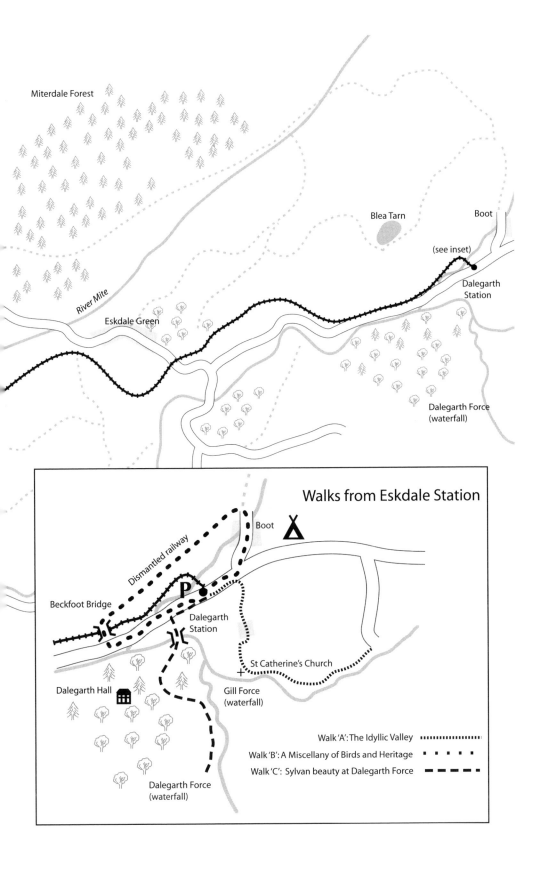

Miterdale Forest

Blea Tarn

Boot

(see inset)

Dalegarth Station

River Mite

Eskdale Green

Dalegarth Force (waterfall)

Walks from Eskdale Station

Dismantled railway

Boot

Beckfoot Bridge

P

Dalegarth Station

Dalegarth Hall

Gill Force (waterfall)

St Catherine's Church

Dalegarth Force (waterfall)

Walk 'A': The Idyllic Valley ••••••••••••••••

Walk 'B': A Miscellany of Birds and Heritage • • • •

Walk 'C': Sylvan beauty at Dalegarth Force ━ ━ ━

in winter by wigeon and teal, seem more placid, though both waders and wildfowl are quick to react to the outline of a peregrine falcon flying over and pandemonium breaks loose.

After passing the picturesque Muncaster Mill, the Mite transforms into a fresh water river and closely follows the railway. The railway itself bisects woodlands and takes a course between Muncaster Fell and the river. Sadly, the red squirrel is now disappearing from the woods alongside La'al Ratty and elsewhere in the Eskdale valley. This is undoubtedly due to the north-wards expansion of the grey squirrel, which now seems to have a firm foothold in the area. Roe deer spend the day lurking in these woods, and creep out at dawn and dusk. They are often revealed by a sudden bark and a conspicuous white rear bobbing away up the side of Muncaster Fell. Any errant deer venturing onto the track is likely to be met with the shrill whistle of the old steam train. There are fanciful stories that one can pick wild flowers from Ratty – an unwise pursuit in the case of the early summer foxgloves that abound on either side of the track – while the slopes of Muncaster Fell are ablaze with the crimson and pink tints of rhododendron.

Listen and look for a variety of birds which may include green and great spotted woodpecker, chiffchaff, blackcap, willow warbler, treecreeper, redstart, nuthatch and long-tailed tit in any of the scattered woodlands lining the valley. Emerging from the woods the peaceful solitude is only likely to be interrupted by the soaring and mewing of buzzards rising on thermals over Muncaster Fell and the bugle-like calls of the resident ravens busy mobbing them. In line-side gardens between Irton Road and Eskdale Green insatiable nuthatch, greenfinch, chaffinch and goldfinch feed on a diet of sunflower hearts and peanuts, while dunnock, blackbird, song thrush and the ubiquitous tiny wren rummage in bushes and garden leaf foliage. Spotted flycatchers can be seen characteristically darting out from cover to catch a fly.

On older properties in Eskdale the familiar swift, swallow, house martin, starling and house sparrow have always lived in harmony with man, but today there are concerns about their current status. On steaming into the terminus station the train crosses over Whillan beck, complete with resident wagtail and dipper. At the end of the line there are views of England's highest mountains, towering above a pastoral landscape with cascading waterfalls and oak woodlands. It is hard to believe that Eskdale was ever anything but a pastoral backwater, but for many centuries from medieval times it was a hive of industry with watermills alongside every river. The three described walks are at their best for bird watching in late April and early May and a careful and observant approach is recommended to enjoy this typical Lakeland valley at its ornithological best.

Walk A: the idyllic valley

The first short walk is alongside the River Esk to Doctor's Bridge and return. It is no hardship but a pleasure to return the same way along a delectable and productive bird watching walk, with further opportunities to catch up on any birds you may have missed.

🚶 **From Dalegarth Station turn left along the narrow road that leads to Hardknott Pass. After a short distance turn right at the Brook House Inn to reach the isolated seventeenth-century St. Catherine's Church, occupying an idyllic site on the north bank of the River Esk. The little graveyard contains an interesting memorial to the memory of Tommy Dobson, founder of the Eskdale and Ennerdale Foxhounds, who died in 1910, as well as some interesting tombstones. Follow the sign to Doctor's Bridge and with the footpath closely paralleling the river continue upstream passing by patches of gorse and bracken. Ahead is an enigmatic structure of two girders that once supported a bridge across the river. This carried a mineral railway from Dalegarth to the mines at Gill Force. View the river before carrying straight on to reach Doctor's Bridge. Return by the same outward route.**

Walk B: a miscellany of birds and heritage

The great thing about bird watching is that birds often live in the most beautiful and interesting places and in close proximity to man. This walk embraces suitable habitat as well as heritage sites where man has lived in close proximity with nature for thousands of years.

🚶 **From Dalegarth Station turn right along the narrow road in the direction of Beckfoot. Ignore the road to the left and turn right through the Beckfoot Access Area. With binoculars poised take a strategically placed seat to view the Whillan Beck. After the bridge but before Stanley Ghyll House, commence walking right along a gravel track through woodland and alongside the railway line. When the railway veers to the right of the old mine cottages, continue straight on along the grassy path, which is actually the track bed of the long-gone, three-foot gauge line that led to Nab Gill Mine at Boot. Cross over a stile, out onto an area of open pasture and fell with rocky slopes.**

❶ On the fellside are traces of the original quarry workings of Nab Gill mine with its terraces, spoil tips and the ruins of the mine's office and Boot station. Interestingly, one of the over-bridges has been rebuilt, with a short section of the three-foot gauge track reinstated. Following the demise of the mining industry the railway was re-laid to the present terminus in 1926.

🚶 **Cross over two small bridges with a ruined farm on the right. At the end of the track turn right into the hamlet of Boot.**

❶ Nestling alongside a picturesque packhorse bridge is a real gem, the last remaining working water mill in the Lake District. There has been a water corn mill working here since medieval times and details of the present building, one of the oldest water mills in England, were first documented in 1578. Brothers Henry and Robert Vicars were the millers, paying an annual rent of eight shillings. The present miller, David King, is on hand to explain the history of the mill and to demonstrate the process of turning grain into flour with a complex arrangement of wooden hoppers, hoists and millstones. Dave may also tell you about the birds that frequent his garden and the interesting woodland habitat besides the mill. Before returning to the train or car, you can take the tour of the mill for a nominal fee and then relax to the pleasant sounds of the mill wheels and the cascading Whillan Beck. Here you can identify a few more birds and even observe *osmunda regalis*, the rare royal fern in its woodland setting before returning to Dalegarth Station.

Walk C: sylvan beauty at Dalegarth Force

This third walk offers more potential for good bird watching. First, to alleviate possible confusion, be aware that Dalegarth Force was formerly known as Stanley Ghyll Force and is named as Stanley Force on Ordnance Survey maps. This is a short walk of sustained charm to Dalegarth Force, situated in the most enchanting sylvan setting and deservedly the most popular walk from Dalegarth Station. The woodland ravine is indeed exquisite and rich in bird life. Also the area around the waterfall is especially good for primitive filmy ferns, which have the distinction of being our smallest native species of fern. They are said to resemble the club mosses, especially when seen growing in native haunts as a tapestry of associated hundreds.

🚶 **Walk right along the road from Dalegarth Station and take the first left at the war memorial. Cross over the River Esk at Trough**

House Bridge (pronounced Tro'fus) while noting the floodwater marks of 1890 and 1962. Go left at the next junction with the 300-year-old Dalegarth Hall in view ahead with its distinctive round Westmorland chimneys. The footpath to Stanley Ghyll is clearly signed.

Keep to the lane until a gate on the left gives access to Stanley Ghyll Wood. From the gate a rough path leads to a stream and continues along the wooded ravine. As the ravine narrows it increasingly becomes more impressive and is crossed over by three footbridges in succession. From the third bridge Dalegarth Force can only partially be seen but this will have to do for those who are not very agile. In order to obtain an uninterrupted view of the waterfall the final approach necessarily involves a scramble from the third bridge and there are obvious dangers to children here – take care before returning to Dalegarth Station via the same route.

Bootle and Silecroft

Stonechat

Sea breezes and gannets along the Cumbria Coastal Way

Start: Bootle railway station
Grid Ref: SD094894
Distance: 7.8 miles (12.6 km)
Time: Allow seven to eight hours with frequent stops for sea watching
Grade: Easy to moderate
General: (See map on page 98.) If arriving by car there are parking, refreshments and toilet facilities at Bootle village, but there are only parking facilities at Bootle Station, which is isolated from the village that it serves. At the time of writing there is no adequate local bus service apart from a Sunday-only service

THIS WALK FOLLOWS A STRETCH of the Cumbria Coastal Way (CCW) between Bootle and Silecroft railway stations. The walk allows for the use of the branch line that runs from Barrow to Carlisle, but it should be noted that both stations are unmanned request stops.

This is an eventful walk through a variety of unspoilt habitats embracing farmland, high alluvial coastal cliffs, a tidal river, lowland heath, coastal shingle and miles of unspoilt sands – with hardly anyone on them. Depending on the weather this exhilarating walk provides opportunities to watch a variety of birds, especially waders and seabirds, while enjoying fabulous seascapes and distant views of the Isle of Man and inland views of Great Gable, with Scafell Pike, England's highest mountain, dominating the skyline.

From Bootle Station turn left, immediately right, and walk west along a rough track passing Broadwater Farm to reach the shore

at Selker Bay. Follow the yellow waymarkers south along the CCW while gradually gaining higher ground on the steep clay cliffs preceding the CCW's descent to the shore. Cross over a stile to enter the Hyton Marsh nature reserve. Leave the reserve by crossing over a footbridge across the River Annas. Stay on the CCW as it crosses over several fields and joins a track at Annaside. Exit the track to Annaside by way of a stile on the right. From here on the walk traverses several fields above Annaside Banks before descending onto a track leading to the shore at Gutterby. There is no public right of way along the cliff or through the fields and one is therefore restricted to the shore. Consideration should be given to tide times for at low tide it is easier to walk on the sands than along the shingle ridge above the high water mark. At Silecroft beach fork left along the one-mile stretch of road to Silecroft railway station and the end of the walk.

❶ Walking along the track to the beach the importance of agriculture and farming to the local community soon becomes evident, but no longer can you assume you will be able to see typical farm-land birds like the lapwing along this stretch of the relatively unspoilt west Cumbrian coast. Barn owl and little owl have enjoyed only mixed breeding success in recent years but may still occasionally be seen in remote areas along the coast. Skylarks may still be seen and heard ascending high into the sky, however, and certain other species are doing well. Peregrine falcon and raven are two examples of birds whose populations have increased and are likely to turn up almost anywhere. Buzzards are today plentiful over the fields and copses. Merlin and kestrel may be seen hunting along the shore and over suitable ground.

At Selker the shingle beach extends in both directions. If your visit coincides with seasonal passage and the right weather conditions – north-westerly/northern gales – there is every chance you might be here for some time doing a sea watch. At a convenient location on the high coastal cliffs take a break to enjoy your sandwiches and a hot drink. A telescope is essential to observe typical wind-blown seabirds like the Manx shearwater shearing above the waves of the Irish Sea. Ornithological literature contains an impressive cast of seabirds seen along the Cumbrian coast. Unusual passage migrants recorded in spring and autumn include sooty shearwater and all four species of skua. Seasonal westerly gales in late summer have led to rare sightings of storm and leach's petrel. Timing is crucial in attempting to see these truly oceanic wanderers of the North Atlantic. One may contemplate their origins on remote and obscure Hebridean islands and whether they will make it to their next mysterious destination. Sadly, on reaching alien coastal waters the tired birds can be predated by a reception committee of herring, lesser black-backed and greater black-backed gulls, where the latter are typically observed dropping shellfish onto the pebbly shoreline.

The estuary of the River Annas is a lonely area of the coast that is seldom visited and is consequently rich in wildlife. Descend the cliffs by the coastal path to reach Hyton reserve, which is next to the river and managed by the Herpelogical Conservation Trust as a breeding site for the endangered natterjack toad. There are only fifty such sites in the whole country and about 50% of these are in Cumbria. During spring these largely nocturnal creatures breed in several of these pools and hunt for invertebrates in the short grazed vegetation. To pick them up or disturb them in any way is an offence and to avoid any encounters with the law they should be left well alone so that the colony of this diminishing species might be given a chance to prosper at one of its few remaining haunts. Biodiversity is further enriched hereabouts by the common blue butterfly, which is invariably to be seen near to its food plant, the bird's foot trefoil. Grayling butterflies flutter over the pebbles where the area above the high tide mark is adorned by both thrift and harebells, adding even more sparkle to the flora of the area.

In April swallows return from tropical Africa to the very same farm outbuildings after circumnavigating many hazards along their route, including the marathon crossing of the Sahara Desert. Indeed during spring and autumn the small flocks of swallows flying along the coast soon become visible signs of migration. As you walk along the Cumbria coastal way during spring time the extensive tracts of gorse and scrub are favoured by whitethroat, meadow pipit, linnet, stonechat and not forgetting the tiny wren. Keep an eye out for them all while simultaneously watching the shoreline for ringed plover and oystercatcher which *still* nest on the quieter stretches of the shingle beach. Regular species likely to be encountered offshore include sandwich tern, fulmar, kittiwake, guillemot, razorbill and various species of wildfowl, especially mallard, red-breasted merganser, eider and wintering flocks of common scoter. During March and April large flocks of red-throated divers drift north and may sometimes be seen in resplendent summer plumage, along with a few great northern and the occasional black-throated diver.

Flocks of gannets are often to be seen in late spring following the mackerel shoals while on fishing expeditions, possibly from the nearest breeding colonies situated at Scar Rocks in the Solway and the huge colony at the Ailsa Craig off the Ayrshire coast. What could be nicer than to experience the sea breezes of a nice spring day while watching these grand white birds flying high above the waves hunting for fish in the blue waters below? Their mastery of the air is superb, especially when with half-closed wings they suddenly dive down before closing their wings entirely and plunge torpedo-like into the water with a terrific splash. One would suspect that their expertise is invariably rewarded with a fish before emergence from the water, catching the breeze and floating away without apparent effort. After the breeding season most of the gannets migrate southward along the Cumbrian coast during August and September.

It should be noted that the coastal walk between Gutterby cliffs and Silecroft beach incorporates a distance of two and a half miles and is restricted entirely to the shore. Above the high water mark and on the sands at low tide large flocks of gulls, cormorants, curlew, oystercatcher, turnstone and ringed plover are invariably present, but perhaps surprisingly on the wader front several key species such as knot and sanderling are not normally represented. The gull and tern flocks that rest on the sands are certainly worth scrutinising for unusual infiltrators. In autumn and winter offshore wildfowl are represented by moderate numbers of mallard, wigeon, red-breasted merganser and common scoter, together with small parties or individual red-throated diver and great crested grebe. Check the old tide line for wintering snow bunting, rock pipit, twite and black redstart, and in spring for the upward posture and white flash of rump of the newly arrived wheatears. Indeed any small birds feeding on the shore are likely suspects and you might even find a rarity.

Adjacent to the caravan park and the road to Silecroft beach is a remnant of heath land which extends to the golf course. The lowland heath is designated as a Site of Special Scientific Interest for its birds and unimproved ground flora, which includes several rare plants such as the tiny adder's tongue fern. The extensive tracts of gorse are worth checking for stonechat and linnet, while the low sedge and small reed bed is the haunt of the sedge warbler. In wintertime flocks of redwing and fieldfare may be seen feeding on berries along the coastal hedgerows. Silecroft is a pretty and peaceful village where time appears to have stood still. Urban birds, such as starling and house sparrow, are still reasonably common here along with flocks of jackdaw and the invasive collared dove.

Waiting for the train, the northbound station platform provides an opportunity to watch the local rookery. Here several pairs nest at low level in sycamore trees next to the platform, and occasionally revisit the colony outside the breeding season.

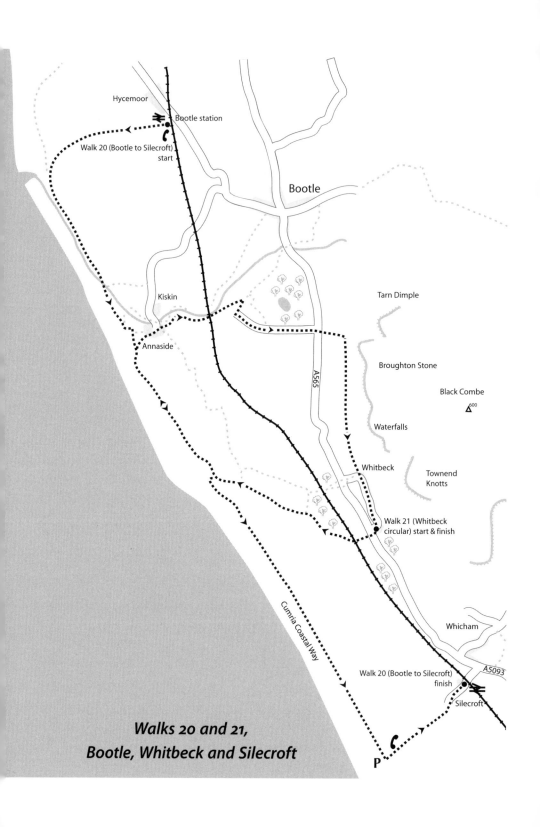

Hycemoor

Bootle station

Walk 20 (Bootle to Silecroft) start

Bootle

Kiskin

Tarn Dimple

Annaside

Broughton Stone

Black Combe
△⁶⁰⁰

Waterfalls

A565

Whitbeck

Townend Knotts

Walk 21 (Whitbeck circular) start & finish

Cumbria Coastal Way

Whicham

A5093

Walk 20 (Bootle to Silecroft) finish

Silecroft

P

*Walks 20 and 21,
Bootle, Whitbeck and Silecroft*

The Whitbeck circular

Lesser black-backed gull

A west Cumbrian coastal and moorland odyssey

Start: Whitbeck Church
Grid Ref: SD119839
Distance: 6.4 miles (10.3 km)
Time: Allow six hours
Grade: Easy
General: Refreshments and toilet facilities at Millom and Bootle. At the time of writing there is no adequate local bus service along the A595 serving the walk, apart from a Sunday only service and therefore the starting point of this walk is best accessed by cycle or motorised transport

THIS CIRCULAR WALK STARTS and finishes at the hamlet of Whitbeck, situated next to the A595 between Silecroft and Bootle. It is designed for the unashamed enjoyment of the unspoilt countryside of west Cumbria and a diversity of contrasting ornithological habitat comprising heath, seashore, moss land, an isolated lowland tarn, quiet country lanes and hedgerows, and the bracken-coated lower slopes of Black Combe. Several species of uncommon birds are present within the localised area, although overall a variety of birds is likely to be seen throughout the walk, including one or two surprises.

Park near to Whitbeck church and follow a substantial track across the A595 to an area known as Gutterby. The track crosses over the railway line and eventually passes Gutterby Farm on the left. Thereafter take the left fork towards the shore where there is an inlet in the substantial clay cliffs. Just before reaching the

shore take the Cumbrian Coastal Way north via the curiously named 'bog hole' to Annaside. At Annaside leave the CCW by turning inland along a minor lane. Walk east along the lane to a farm on your right and carry straight on along a footpath through the field that parallels the River Annas on your left. Cross over Mitergill Beck and go under the railway bridge. Continue walking along a narrow path with the River Annas on your left before eventually striking off right to a minor lane that leads south of Barfield Tarn to Holmgate Farm.

(※) After viewing Barfield Tarn on your left, walk along the lane to a junction with the main road (A595). Cross over the road and continue straight ahead along a footpath that bisects a couple of fields to a bridleway that passes along the lower fringe of Black Combe. Turn right along the path and continue along the lower fringe of Black Combe below the picturesque waterfall of Millergill beck. After passing through the hamlet of Whitbeck you will reach Whitbeck church that marks the starting and finishing point of the walk.

❶ Walking to the shore between Whitbeck and Gutterby look out for typical birds of the area, such as song thrush and other members of the thrush family, as well as dunnock, house sparrow, pied and grey wagtail, long-tailed tit and wren. During summer, swift and hirundines – swallow, sand martin and house martin – enhance the rural scene. In autumn the 'chack chack' call of the first fieldfares come close behind the last swallow of the summer, and as winter progresses roving flocks of fieldfares and redwings may be seen stripping the berries off trees along this remote lane.

A few pairs of skylarks may still be heard singing beautifully over unimproved coastal fields and remnants of heaths. In early April curlews leave their winter haunts along the shore and may by found on the fells and in lowland fields. With its namesake call and long curving beak there are not many things more evocative than the sight and sound of a curlew flying over, except perhaps hearing the first cuckoo in spring.

Listening to Vaughan William's 'A Lark Ascending' makes one ponder how much longer the skylark will be the prima donna of the great outdoors. Diminishing bird populations make a compelling environmental statement and something must be done to balance the competing interests of agriculture and birds.

The quiet mosses of the Cumbrian coast are known to attract barn owl and at the right time of the day a careful scan of the heath alongside the railway might reward you with a sighting of this usually silent and ghostly creature before it finally fades into oblivion. Unfortunately, along the Cumbrian coast there is substantial evidence that local barn conversions continue to present a particular threat to their existence, together with the general degeneration of their habitat. To counter this, nest boxes are being placed in suitable buildings.

The walk follows a short section of the Cumbria Coastal Way between Gutterby and Annaside,* where turnstone, oystercatcher, curlew and ringed plover may be seen on the beach. Winter and spring are good times to watch for red-throated divers, great crested grebe and common scoter, while in summer the flocks of gannet may be seen fishing offshore. Stonechat, linnet, wheatear, meadow pipit, skylark, willow warbler, whitethroat and sometimes grasshopper warbler frequent the coastal strands of gorse and open areas. During winter peregrine and merlin are quite likely to be seen anywhere along the shore. Along the coast and adjacent agricultural land crows and gulls are represented by raven, carrion crow, rook, jackdaw, black headed, herring, common and lesser black-back gull.

On leaving the Cumbria Coastal Way and turning inland a diversity of habitat begins to unfold. Buzzards may often be seen hereabouts, both soaring over the fells and perching on fence posts. Grey wagtails haunt the River Annas, where dippers are only occasionally seen. The walk up the river also provides an opportunity to see sedge warbler, heron, reed bunting, curlew and, if you are lucky, snipe. Of the summer visitors blackcap, whitethroat and willow warbler sing beautifully in spring and it is their song that helps to locate them. Also in the extensive hedgerows and shrub will be long-tailed tit and other members of the same family, as well as chaffinch, goldfinch and possibly lesser redpoll and bullfinch, all of which are likely to tempt the principal predators of small birds, sparrowhawk and merlin.

During June and July Barfield Tarn is usually a disappointment for the birdwatcher, holding only a few species such as mute swan, motley mallards and greylag geese. Late autumn and winter brings tufted duck, teal, pochard, goldeneye, goosander, moorhen and coot. In spring and autumn a migrating osprey is possible and passage migrants such as greenshank also drop in to feed. Although there is little vegetation for nesting birds what is important is that it provides an opportunity for migrating hirundines passing along the Cumbrian coast to feed on the innumerable insects flying over the surface of the water.

---

* For further details of shore birds to be seen along a corresponding section of a similar walk see page 96.

The old fashioned country lane that leads to the A595 is something of a time capsule, as evidenced by an abundance of honeysuckle, foxgloves and viper's bugloss, and at the time of writing the lush vegetation and hedgerow was still a haunt of the delightful yellowhammer and several species of warbler. At the right time of day barn owls may be seen hereabouts and in the vicinity of Barfield Tarn.

On approaching the lower fringes of Black Combe scan the fellside for merlin, buzzard, peregrine and kestrel. Skylark, stonechat and yellowhammer haunt the lower bracken-covered slopes of the Combe. The latter is likely to be located in a small tree or on an elevated perch in the bracken making a 'chit' alarm call or delivering its song, likened to 'a little bit of bread and no cheese', and what a super bird this is, resplendent with bright lemon below and orange-rufous colouration above. The stonechat has in recent years expanded its choice of breeding sites to upland areas but sadly the whinchat has markedly declined and one can no longer rely on seeing the latter. At Whitbeck kestrels hover on the wind looking for their favoured prey of small mammals, and ravens may be heard croaking high above or flying alongside the fell. At Whitbeck you reach the end of the walk but if you are feeling particularly energetic and want to climb Black Combe then save it for another day and the next described walk.

The Black Combe circuit

Peregrine

Mountain isolation and birds

Start and finish: Silecroft railway station
Grid Ref: SD130820
Distance: 8 miles (12.9 km)
Time: Allow four to five hours
Grade: Moderate to strenuous
General: Car parking, toilets and refreshments at Silecroft (PT)

THIS IS AN ABSORBING circular fell walk with the backdrop of the south-west Cumbrian mountains. The isolated outcrop of Black Combe's rugged grandeur can be seen dominating the landscape from many areas around Morecambe Bay. The walk extends from Silecroft to the summit of Black Combe, which stands at 1,970 feet high, and continues as a circular walk around the fell, providing an opportunity to see a range of upland birds. For safety reasons take a compass or GPS, and do not attempt the ascent when there is the slightest hint of poor visibility. The birds will then take a bit of finding and you might even get lost or worse. Be warned that east of the rounded summit there are rocky slopes with high crags and screes. In a more placid and idyllic setting the walk passes close to St Mary's Church, Whicham, situated in the delightful Whicham Valley. The church has several interesting features including a Norman arch, medieval bells and font, and the story of Tom Mayson of Silecroft who won the Victoria Cross during the Great War.

From Silecroft Station walk through the village and follow the main road left towards Whicham, taking the first turning right at the road junction. Turn first left along a picturesque lane past Whicham Church to the start of the climb up the south-west face of Black Combe. After passing the white house (left), known as

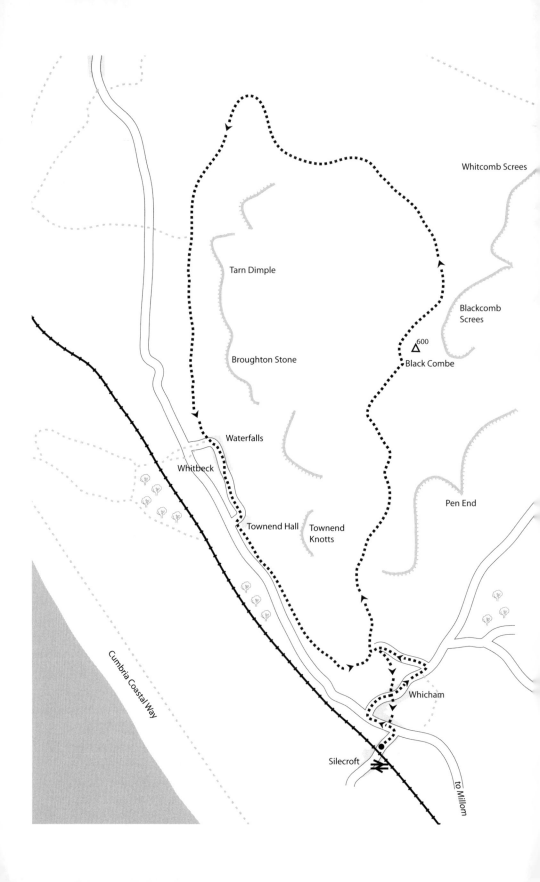

Whitcomb Screes

Tarn Dimple

Blackcomb Screes

Broughton Stone

$\triangle$ 600
Black Combe

Waterfalls

Whitbeck

Pen End

Townend Hall

Townend
Knotts

Cumbria Coastal Way

Whicham

Silecroft

to Millom

Kirkbank, cross over a stile and follow a grassy track up through
the lower slopes of the valley of Moor Gill Beck to a short steep
stretch before gaining Townend Knotts. This is the hardest bit
and from here on the pace is more relaxing before reaching a
subsidiary peak and eventually an arrow of stones pointing right
to the summit trig point.

⊛ From the summit the easiest way down is, of course, to retrace
your steps directly to the Whicham Valley. Alternatively, continue
an extended circular walk by first walking east along the track
above Black Combe screes, before veering north west past disused
quarries and a sheepfold. The defined path then swings south,
with unfolding panoramic views of England's highest mountains
and the Cumbrian coast north to St Bees. After crossing over
Hallfoss and Holegill Becks and skirting the craggy slopes along
the western side of the fell, the track continues along the lower
fringe of Black Combe below the picturesque waterfall of Millergill
beck. After passing through the hamlet of Whitbeck you will reach
Whitbeck Church and join the main A591. Walk along the border
of this main road to a footpath on the left that leads back to
Kirkbank. From this point the walk again ascends the bracken-
covered slopes of Black Combe to a junction with the path from
Kirkbank to the summit. The final stage of the walk descends past
Kirkbank, and immediately thereafter turn right along a public
footpath that bisects fields and crosses over the A591 before
reaching the end of the walk at Silecroft railway station.

ⓘ The lane leading from Whicham Church and the lower slopes of Black
Combe may produce linnet, blackcap, willow warbler, long-tailed tit,
goldcrest, stonechat, meadow pipit, skylark, pied wagtail and small
numbers of yellowhammers. In spring that past master of song, the
skylark, may be heard singing high above the slopes of the fell, and
meadow pipits still rise and fall with a charmingly fresh crescendo.

At the summit any lack of birds may be compensated for by the
fine 360° views to be enjoyed and the splendid solitude of mountain
isolation. To the south west the view of Blackpool Tower and the
coastal plain of the Wyre estuary at Fleetwood extends north across
Morecambe Bay to Walney Island, the Duddon estuary, and the Lake
District's western and central mountains and valleys. On a clear day it
may be possible to make out the mountains of North Wales, Dumfries
and Galloway, the Isle of Man's Snaefell and the Irish coast.

North east of the trig point takes in the panoramic view over screes, crags and Black Combe's eastern buttress of White Combe. This is an excellent place to enjoy the tranquillity of the mountain with a timely meal break. At the same time listen and look out for upland raptors typically represented by peregrine, kestrel, buzzard and sometimes merlin. Peregrine and merlin are respectively our largest and smallest breeding species of falcon and both specialise in taking birds that frequent Black Combe and the lowland coastal fields, while kestrel and buzzard both have a preference for mammals and sometimes carrion. The familiar calls of jackdaws may often be heard in this habitat, which is shared with meadow pipit and sometimes wheatear. A chance sighting of a ring ouzel in the higher cloughs, quarries or crags would really make your day, so be ever watchful for this much sought after species of mountain blackbird.

Keep your eyes open too for buzzards, often known as 'the tourist's eagle'. It is now officially regarded as the most abundant bird of prey in the UK and breeding takes place in most counties. Likewise, the largest member of the crow family, the raven, is now common in Lakeland and may be encountered anywhere on this walk. Recognition of its distinct croaking call while flying high above is an important aid to identification, together with its characteristic flight profile.

The instantly recognisable call of the male cuckoo demands attention and is warmly regarded as one of the harbingers of spring. The cuckoo has sadly declined in many parts of Britain and these days you would be fortunate to see or hear one on this walk. The male calls both in flight and when perched but despite this it is often difficult to locate. When calling from a perch he has a very characteristic pose. He bows forward, lowering the head and drooping the wings while fanning the elevated tail. Nowadays the local whinchat population on Black Combe seems to have been superseded by the ubiquitous and resident stonechat.

Grey wagtails add the finishing touches to the cascading waterfall in the picturesque Clough of Mitergill Beck. Hedgerows and gardens at Whitbeck are also the haunt of great spotted woodpecker, goldcrest, titmice and siskin. However, garden feeding stations are not always the safe haven for birds that they seem. Certain predators will exploit small birds wherever they gather to feed, so like the birds keep ceaseless watch for that superbly adapted hunter the resident sparrowhawk, which is likely to turn up almost anywhere when least expected.

A circular walk at Millom

Pintail

Borwick Rails and Hodbarrow

Start: Start and finish at Millom railway station
Grid Ref: SD172802
Distance: 4.4 miles (7 km)
Time: Allow six hours
Grade: Easy
General: The Barrow to Carlisle railway serves Millom (not Sundays), but there is no adequate bus service. Toilets, car parking and refreshments are at Millom and Haverigg. There is disabled access to Hodbarrow

THIS IS ANOTHER RICH ornithological circular walk, embracing a diversity of seaside habitat and set against a backdrop of the south-west Cumbrian mountains. Millom is steeped in local history and industrial archaeology and nestles in the beautiful landscape that is synonymous with this quiet corner of the western Lake District. Millom iron works was the town's principal employer until its closure in 1968. Today the old harbour at Borwick Rails plays host to birds rather than to the Victorian sailing ships that plied their trade and the more recent Royal Navy ships that came here to be scrapped. The site provides excellent views of the estuary across to Sandscale, Walney Island and the mountains of south and west Cumbria. Nowadays, Millom is transferring its allegiance from its industrial past to tourism, including the provision of facilities for observing wildlife and bird watching.

The main focus of the walk is the RSPB reserve at Hodbarrow. The reserve is an area of scrub and marsh around a large freshwater lagoon and is an important Site of Special Scientific Interest. The reserve has much to offer throughout the year, although is probably at its best from late April to early July. The wide range of habitats and ease of access allow a full day's birding

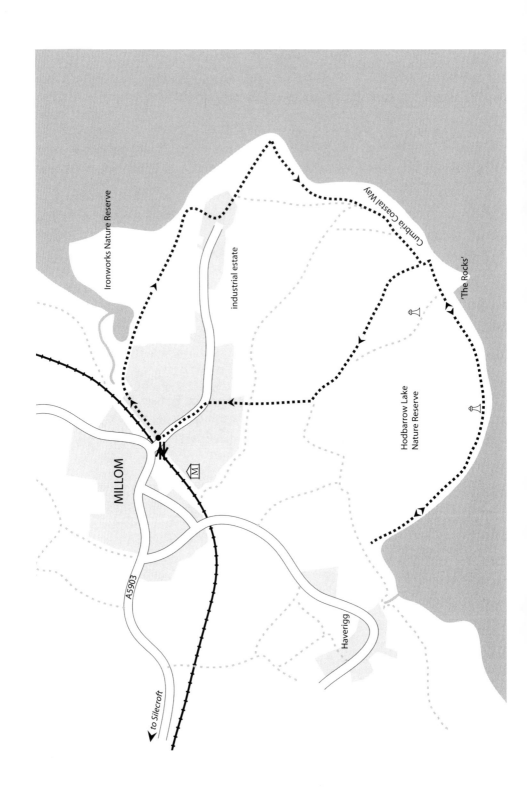

and a leisurely approach. The reserve is the flooded site of a former iron
ore mine and is enclosed by the sea wall, which was built to protect the
haematite iron-ore mine. For c. 120 years iron ore was mined, and at the peak
of the industry around 1,000 men worked in the mine and the associated
iron works. The original sea wall was replaced by the present sea wall, which
was completed in 1905. Looking over the present peaceful scene it is hard to
imagine the hive of activity that continued until 1968. Once pumping stopped
the present lagoon was created. Most of the industrial archaeology was
removed in the 1970s and 1980s, but two lighthouse towers and the walls of
a windmill remain. Near the stump of an old windmill the cliffs at Hodbarrow
Point are worth exploring at low tide for they are home to that localised but
hardy maritime fern, the sea spleenwort.

(※) **From Millom railway station turn left into Lancashire Road and
follow the Cumbria Coastal Way along a disused railway line
to Millom Iron Works Local nature reserve. Continue along the
Cumbria Coastal Way to the headland at Hodbarrow Point and
onto the RSPB Hodbarrow nature reserve. An alternative shorter
route to the reserve may be taken on foot or by car or bicycle and
may be considered suitable for the disabled. However, be warned
that the track to the reserve between Mainsgate Road and the sea
wall is rough, making it necessary to take care when driving. From
Millom Station follow Devonshire Road and after the town centre
turn right into Mainsgate Road. Follow the brown tourist signs to
the RSPB reserve and park on the sea wall alongside the lagoon.**

❶ The first stage of the extended walk to Hodbarrow Reserve passes
through the Millom Iron Works Local Nature Reserve and Borwick
Rails pier, located next to the Duddon Estuary. This was the site of
Millom iron works and exemplifies how a former major industrial
site can be put to excellent use. The site has reverted to nature
and plant communities have developed on the slag and disturbed
ground, typically represented by bee orchids and yellow wort, while
the grasslands host several species of butterfly. Natterjack toads are
engaging creatures that breed in several pools where dragonflies hawk
over the water during the summer months looking to lay their eggs.

Again the tide is crucial, and although birds are more active on a
rising tide, high and low tide offer something different. Have lunch at
the top of the slag heap, for if you have planned it right by now the
tide will have started to ebb and there will be both water and exposed
mud. The reserve attracts warblers, rock pipit, meadow pipit, stonechat
and skylark. In spring expect to see both the smallest (little tern) and

largest members of the tern family (sandwich tern), as well as common and the occasional Arctic tern, often euphemistically known as 'comic terns', or perhaps more elegantly, sea swallows. Up to four species of tern may be seen flying to and from the breeding colony at Hodbarrow. With any luck the young birds from this colony will have fledged by the end of June and be on the wing, thus presenting a few more identification challenges. Outside of the breeding season the Duddon channel and mudflats are also the haunt of cormorant, heron, redshank, greenshank, curlew, oystercatcher, lapwing, dunlin, common sandpiper, red-breasted merganser, mallard, pintail, goldeneye, teal, wigeon, eider, great crested grebe, cormorant, heron and occasional red-throated diver, guillemot and razorbill.

(ℵ) **Skirt the seaward side of the large lagoon by walking along the sea wall to a public hide. Continue along the sea wall (Cumbria Coastal Way) to the end of the lagoon, or alternatively go into Haverigg to obtain refreshments then retrace your steps back along the sea wall towards Hodbarrow Point. After the lagoon take a public path left that leads between two smaller lagoons onto Mainsgate Road and back to Millom railway station**

ℹ️ Hodbarrow Point, known locally as 'The Rocks', is noteworthy for the migrants taking advantage of the diversity of small cliffs, foreshore, scrub, copses and the lagoons that are integral to the RSPB's Hodbarrow Nature Reserve. The reserve itself can be viewed while walking round it and from a hide located on the sea wall. Today the reserve fulfils important criteria as a site for passage of wildfowl and waders and as a breeding site for them. Of particular importance, however, is the specially protected tern colony that incorporates up to four of the five British species, including a large colony of sandwich terns. The latter species is, however, rather fickle in their choice of nest site and often moves location after a bad breeding season. Black-headed gulls nest every year and seem oblivious to any water skiing activities.

On the approach to the hide watch out for breeding ringed plover and oystercatchers, taking great care not to stand on their nests. The island and water in front of the hide is usually full of birds. In spring the terns take pride of place, especially the densely packed sandwich terns, with lesser numbers of common and Arctic tern spread more thinly. Right in front of the hide are the delightful little terns, initially difficult to pick out on the bare shingle areas. A careful count though will usually produce between 30 and 50 pairs. The best spectacle is when a 'dread' occurs, sometimes caused by a potential predator and at other times for no apparent reason. This causes all the terns to take to flight and vent their vocal concern in a short-lived cacophony of sound. The amount of activity depends on the time of your visit in relation to the breeding cycle. Early in the season there is much displaying as pairs and territories are established. This is followed by a quieter period as incubation takes place. Then, as the young hatch, there is a period of constant to-ing and fro-ing with food for the young birds, culminating in the fledging of many young birds in a successful season. Other breeding birds include lapwing, ringed plover, oystercatcher, lesser black-backed and herring gulls, eider, tufted duck, merganser and greylag. Many pairs of great crested grebe build their nests comprising a great mound of water-weed and other debris. After hatching, try to count the bizarrely striped young as they hitch a ride on their parents' backs.

Waders regularly feed on the muddy margins or use the island as a high tide roost. These are mainly estuarine waders with the best variety during spring and autumn passage periods. Dunlin, knot, redshank, turnstone, ringed plover and black-tailed godwit are the commonest, but ruff, curlew sandpiper, little stint, green sandpiper, greenshank and spotted redshank also occur in smaller numbers. Numbers of wildfowl are always present, especially diving ducks, which favour the deeper water. Mergansers use the lagoon as a moulting site in summer, although numbers are somewhat lower than in former years when up to 350 were regular. Of the surface feeders, wigeon and teal are the commonest, while gadwall, shoveler and pintail are less frequent. The proximity to the sea means that sea duck, including scaup, long tail duck and common scoter, occur spasmodically. In spring watch out for little gulls hawking insects over the water, and easterly winds can bring an influx of black terns.

Watching the estuary from the top of the sea wall gives a good view of the main low tide feeding areas that are good for shore waders and wildfowl. During the breeding season there is a constant passage of terns from the sea to the lagoon, many carrying sand eels that in spring are presented to the female by the males – the avian equivalent of a box of chocolates! The raucous call of the gull-like sandwich tern is heard constantly and the delightfully light and acrobatic flight of the little tern is a joy to watch. Meadow pipits and wheatears often flit in front of you.

On an incoming tide flocks of oystercatcher, dunlin, knot, curlew and redshank pass close by while flying to their high tide roosts. The spectacle is best from late autumn to early spring but there is always something to see. When the tide is in, watch out for seabirds including gannets, skuas and divers. As well as the obligatory gulls, watch out for the occasional white-winged glaucous gull – always to be regarded as quite a find. Peregrine, kestrel and merlin are three species of falcon that are commonly observed, especially in winter. The merlin is our smallest bird of prey and may be found on the fells in summer and open country in winter. They are specialist hunters and with their fast, twisting flight are superbly adapted to take passerines like the meadow pipits that visit the coastal fields around Millom and the rocks at Hodbarrow.

During autumn and winter interesting passerines are possible anywhere on the reserve, including snow bunting and black redstart. After passing by the main lagoon and Hodbarrow Point there are several side paths between the lagoons that are well worth exploring, especially in spring. The scrub areas are good for breeding warblers with numbers of whitethroat, willow, sedge and garden warblers, chiffchaff, blackcap and the two less common species, grasshopper warbler and lesser whitethroat. It is an excellent place to learn or brush up on your song identification. You will notice subtle differences in the habitats of these warblers, with chiffchaff, blackcap and lesser whitethroat mainly in the more mature areas of scrub and the others in the shorter, bushier areas. Other common breeders include reed bunting and linnet. Several rarities have occurred over the years, including white-rumped sandpiper, Kentish plover, Richard's pipit and icterine warbler.

The smaller lagoons on either side of the track and the eastern end of the large lagoon are good for large numbers of coot, red-breasted merganser, great crested grebe, surface feeding and diving ducks, little grebe, greylag, and, at passage periods, freshwater waders including green sandpiper and greenshank This general area and the fields to the south of the track are well used by barn owl, mainly at dawn and dusk but especially in winter they can be seen hunting at any time of day. The extensive tracts of gorse are regularly favoured by stonechats.

Botanically the inner part of the sea wall is very interesting, with many common limestone plants, such as dark red helleborine, bloody cranesbill and pyramidal orchid. In June and early July the area of open ground to the east of the large lagoon is greatly enhanced by colonies of northern marsh, pyramidal and bee orchids. Several species of butterfly are attracted to the reserve. The red admiral, small tortoiseshell, painted lady, dark green fritillary and the grayling all add a touch of colour as they flit around their favoured food plants. Natterjack toads breed in several of the smaller pools. At high tide do not be too surprised to find an Atlantic grey seal watching you or maybe even a common seal. The latter is badly named, however, for it is not nearly so common as the grey seal around the British coast.

South Walney Nature Reserve

Sanderling

Start and finish: The reserve car park
Grid Ref: SD204633
Distance: 4.4 miles (7 km) (reserve area only)
Time: Allow 4–6 hours
Grade: Easy
General: Toilets at the car park, other facilities in Barrow-in-Furness

THIS WALK PROVIDES EXCELLENT bird watching all year round. It takes in the sand dunes and gravel pits of the reserve, all set against the ever changing world of the tidal regime. The walk concentrates on the reserve with its excellent paths and hides but a possible extension for those wanting a longer walk is included. Watching is most rewarding when the tide is above 8.5 metres and it is best to arrive at least two hours before high tide.

Park in the reserve car park and obtain your day permit from the kiosk. (An information board gives details of recent sightings.) Take the well-marked trail down the inner side of the island visiting first the Observation Hide and then the Central Marsh Hide before going to the Pier Hide overlooking Light House Bay.

During the breeding season from February to early August the numbers of large gulls is somewhat overwhelming to first-time visitors. Old hands know to wear old clothes and a hat, for you never know what they will drop on you! The breeding population has recently been estimated at c. 15,000 pairs, of which lesser black-backed gulls make up two thirds and herring gulls the rest, except for about 70

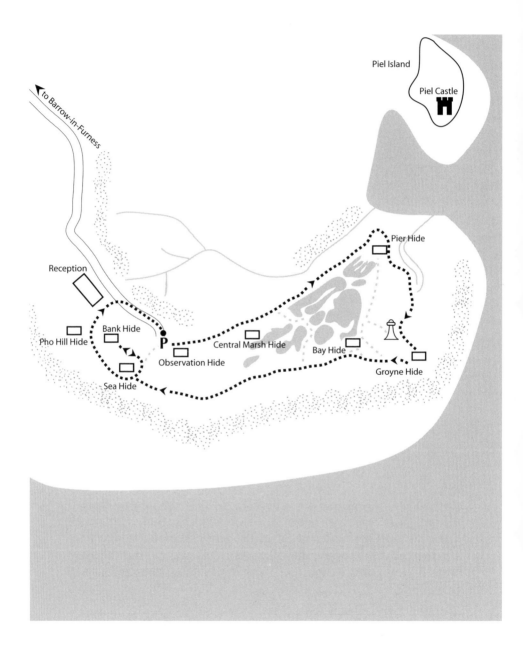

Piel Island

Piel Castle

to Barrow-in-Furness

Reception

Pho Hill Hide

Bank Hide

P

Observation Hide

Sea Hide

Central Marsh Hide

Bay Hide

Pier Hide

Groyne Hide

pairs of great black-backed gulls. It is a stimulating experience to walk through the colony with the gulls rising before you and quickly settling behind you, with a cacophony of sounds and smells. May and June are the best time to visit when you can see nests at all stages of development. A clue to the food preferences of the birds can be gained from the remains around the nest; some specialise in prey from the intertidal area while others prefer to visit the rubbish tips of Barrow. You will have no problem seeing the two common species for they are everywhere, even though the herring gull population has seen recent marked declines both locally and nationally. The greater black-backs prefer the islands and spits within the gravel pit complex, their much darker mantles and larger size making them obvious.

Nesting among the gulls are large numbers of Eiders. At one time up to 1500 pairs nested at Walney but predation by foxes, and possibly over exploitation by man of their main food source of mussels, has caused a decline to around 200 pairs in recent years. From late winter through to early spring rafts of birds float offshore. The highly coloured males court the drab females with much head bobbing, jerking and a lovely cooing note. As the season progresses and most females are incubating, the display gets even more frantic as several males surround each still unpaired female in a bid to win her favours. In the groups are many adolescent males, not in full plumage and not old enough to breed.

Eiders nest on the ground among vegetation or tidal debris and some can be quite exposed, with the cryptic plumaged (camouflaged) female undertaking all the incubation. When hatched the young are led into the sea and here the ducklings mix with other broods to form crèches in an attempt to protect them from marauding gulls.

During the walk along the shore scan the flocks of oystercatchers, curlew, dunlin and redshank which are eventually pushed off by the rising tide when they flight towards the high tide roosts at the south of the island, or to Sheep Island to the north. Numbers of ringed plover and turnstone roost at high tide along the shingle beaches. Redshank and dunlin will also roost there but are much more likely to leave as you approach. On the flowing tide large flocks of eiders and shelduck, along with red-breasted mergansers, also head towards the spit at the south of the island. In winter the sand dunes often hold flocks of twite and other finches, including goldfinch and linnet.

In spring and summer look out for South Walney's special plants, many of them extremely colourful and with intriguing names such as henbane, viper's bugloss hound's tongue, mullein, bloody cranesbill, and yellow horned poppy, along with the delightful wild pansy which flowers from May until November.

The Central Marsh Hide comes into its own at passage periods and in winter when waders and wildfowl visit the shallow pools. To the west of the track are the old gravel workings and the oyster farm. The water areas, islands and spits hold grebes, wildfowl, especially merganser and goldeneye, but also surface-feeding ducks such as wigeon, shoveler and teal and waders such as greenshank and spotted redshank. In recent years numbers of little egrets have taken up residence, roosting in the gravel pits and moving out to feed in the salt marsh creeks and intertidal areas.

The Pier Hide looks out towards the distant Piel and Foulney islands. In the foreground are the entrance to Lighthouse Bay and the large spit which forms the south of the island. Here at high tide congregate large numbers of oystercatcher and eider, along with smaller numbers of grey plover, sanderling, turnstone, knot, dunlin, cormorant, wigeon and a motley collection of gulls. Between autumn and spring careful watching of the bay and the water towards Piel Island usually reveals red-throated, and occasionally other, divers, along with great crested grebes and common scoter and occasionally long-tailed ducks and scaup. Watch out for the ravens which now breed and frequent Piel Castle.

⦿ **Leave the hide as the tide ebbs and head along the path past the lighthouse and out to the Groyne Hide, then back and to the Bay Hide and along the path to the Sea Hide.**

❶ Here one can view both the Walney Channel and the Irish Sea and watch for birds passing along the coast including terns, sea duck, waders and wildfowl. Peregrine and merlin are regular, often disturbing the roosting waders and providing a superb spectacle. The walk towards the Sea Hide takes you through the densest part of the gullery and is also a good area for nesting eiders. In winter short-eared owl frequent the grassy areas, as do flocks of twite and occasionally small parties of snow bunting. The Bay Hide overlooks the gravel workings which hold mainly diving ducks and some waders.

The Sea Hide, as its name suggests, is ideal for sea watching in comfort. Winds with a westerly element during spring and autumn produce the best results; patience is required but hopefully you will be rewarded with sights of gannet, kittiwake, fulmar, guillemot, razor bill, red-throated divers, Arctic terns, Manx shearwater, great and Arctic skuas, common and velvet scoters and occasionally leach's and storm petrels.

⊛ **From the Sea Hide follow the path to the Bank Hide and back to the car park, or alternatively return to the Sea Hide and follow the path to the Pho Hill Hide and back past the gate pond to the car park.**

❶ The Bank Hide gives a good chance of seeing freshwater waders such as snipe, ruff and black-tailed godwit, as well as wildfowl including shoveler, gadwall and teal. You are never quite certain what might turn up and there are several records of grey phalarope on this small pool.

The bushes round the cottages and kiosk are well worth checking although you need to be a member of The Walney Bird Observatory to drive the Heligoland trap (a large, building-sized, funnel shaped structure of wire mesh used to trap birds for ringing, etc.). An amazing variety of passerines have been recorded over the years at South Walney, from bluethroat to melodious warbler.

Depending on the time of year, and of course which birds are present, a visit to South Walney can take the best part of a day. A further option for those who want to explore is to take the road and public footpaths along the sea shore to reach the small hamlet of Biggar Bank, then cross the island and return to South Walney along the Irish Sea coast. This is the longer walk, a shorter walk is also shown on the map taking in the fields and seashore just outside the reserve.

On the longer walk, high tide wader and wildfowl roosts can be found at Bent How, Scar End and Snab points. Species composition is similar to South Walney but Bent How can be good for sanderling and small numbers of purple sandpipers. The hedges and gorse clumps attract breeding stonchat and linnet, and at passage periods look out for migrant wheatear, whinchat and warblers. The many fields or patches of rough grass still attract skylarks and at migration times flocks of meadow pipits and, when flooded, wildfowl and waders. Twite and linnet regularly frequent the rough ground and coastline in winter, as occasionally do small parties of snow buntings.

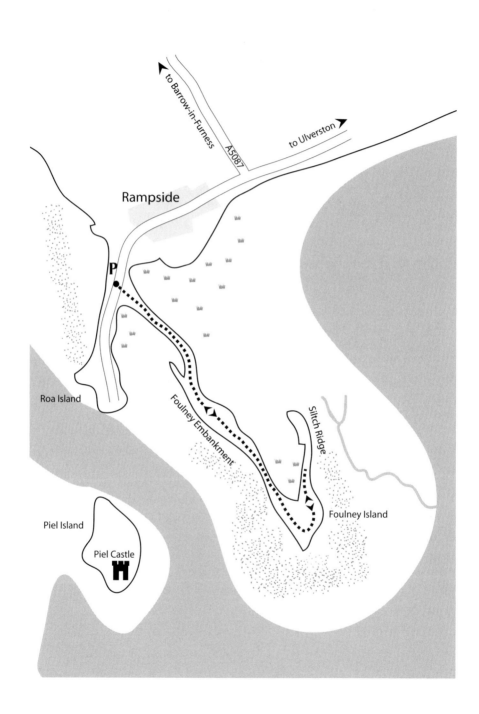

to Barrow-in-Furness

to Ulverston

A5087

Rampside

P

Roa Island

Foulney Embankment

Slitch Ridge

Foulney Island

Piel Island

Piel Castle

Foulney Island

Ringed plover

Start and finish: Rampside

Grid Ref: SD235661

Distance: 3.1 miles (5 km)

Time: Allow up to six hours and aim to be crossing the causeway to Foulney at around two to three hours before high tide

Grade: Easy

General: Carefully study the tide table, for on high tides Foulney Island may be cut off from the mainland. Car parking, toilet and refreshment facilities at Rampside and Roa Island; railway stations at Roose and Barrow; bus service between Ulverston and Barrow (PT)

FOULNEY IS ONE OF FOUR small islands lying between mainland Furness and the southern tip of Walney Island. Foulney Island is attached to the Roa Island causeway by its own causeway, originally built to prevent silting of the Piel channel. Foulney has long been known as a bird island and the earliest bird records come from the 1840s when roseate and common terns nested in roughly equal number and little and arctic terns were also present.

🚶 **From the village of Rampside follow the road towards Roa Island. If arriving by car, park in the small car park on the left-hand side of the causeway. From here take the causeway path onto the island. Once on the island please keep to the path during the breeding season, to avoid crushing eggs and disturbing nesting birds on the beaches and grasslands.**

❶ Foulney Island is owned by Broughton Estates and leased to the
Cumbria Wildlife Trust, who have managed the island as a reserve since
appointing its first warden in 1963. The island is uninhabited except by
the warden who supervises the reserve during the summer. The Wild
Birds Foulney Order (1980) gives the island legal protection and prevents
access to the Slitch Ridge tern colony between 1 April and 15 August
each year. Dogs are not permitted on the reserve during this period.

Today Foulney is still essentially a bird island and during the
summer its main conservation interests are its breeding terns and
nesting shore birds. Tern colonies are fickle and if they have a
disastrous breeding season they often desert an area and move
elsewhere. In recent years around fifty pairs of Arctic tern and fifteen
little terns pairs have nested with variable success. Sandwich terns
used to nest here in good numbers but in recent years they have
moved to Hodbarrow where they have several alternative sites, so the
chances of them moving back to Foulney look rather remote. The tern
colony tends to move from year to year but the warden fences off
their chosen site to avoid disturbance. By sitting a little distance away
you can watch the comings and goings in the colony. The Arctic tern
prefer the vegetated shingle areas but the little tern scorns any cover
and nests on the open shingle. You can also study the differences in
flight of these two species, with the Arctic tern's leisurely spring flight
contrasting with the rapid and erratic flight of the smaller little tern.

Mussel beds just offshore make Foulney, along with South Walney,
an ideal breeding place for eiders, and although numbers still nest
they have declined in recent years due mainly, it is thought, to the
commercial exploitation of the mussels, the main food of this species.
Eiders are endearing to watch, especially during spring when the
courtship display of the male can be seen and heard around the
island. Several males will often serenade one female by throwing their
heads back and making their fabulous cooing calls. Female eiders are
renowned for sitting tight on their eggs, allowing a close approach, but
do not disturb them as predatory gulls move in quickly to take any
unguarded eggs. Once hatched the young are taken to the sea where
several broods often amalgamate to form a large crèche, very often
of young of different ages and sizes. Other breeding species include
numbers of oystercatcher, ringed plover, nesting mainly on the extensive
shingle beaches, and skylarks on the grassy centre of the island.

As the terns leave Foulney in late summer with their newly fledged
young, thousands of waders and wildfowl journey here either to
winter or pass further south. Foulney, with its large area of adjacent
intertidal sand flats and mussel beds, provides a rich food source for

these voyagers. Over high tide they roost in numbers on the spits and beaches, allowing excellent bird watching, but take care not to disturb them. Regular species include curlew, bar-tailed godwit, knot, grey plover, turnstone, dunlin, oystercatcher, eider and shelduck. During passage period numbers of sanderling and ringed plover occur, with the largest numbers in late May. These are birds bound for their breeding areas in Greenland so they have many hundreds of miles to travel before they can start breeding. In the case of the ringed plover, their British cousins, there may already be young to care for.

Peregrine and merlin regularly pursue the roosting wader flocks, while short-eared owl and kestrel hunt for small mammals in the long grass. A small and increasing party of dark-bellied brent geese is present each winter. They are joined by large numbers of wigeon and shelduck, many of which feed on the zostera or eelgrass on the intertidal area. At high tide large numbers of wildfowl congregate on the water in the bay formed by Foulney and Roa islands.

At high tide it is well worth scanning the sea for grebes, divers and sea ducks. The most regular are great crested grebe, red-throated diver and goldeneye. But many rarities have occurred including slavonian grebe, black-throated diver and long-tailed duck. Paserines frequenting the shingle have included rock pipit, twite and shore lark,

South Walney and Foulney comprise one of the best areas of vegetated shingle in Britain. Above the high water mark is a zone of bare shingle with scattered plants of sea kale, yellow horned poppy, curled dock and sea campion, plants which have special adaptations enabling them to survive where freshwater is scarce. Diversity increases with distance from the sea and bird's foot trefoil, biting stonecrop, herb Robert and scurvy grass complement the ground flora. Salt marsh is developing in the bay between the main island and Slitch Ridge and is slowly replacing the grass *spartina*, or cord grass, which has colonised large areas of sand flats. Other small areas of salt marsh support sea purslane, sea lavender and glasswort.

Foulney has an interesting population of butterflies and moths. Grayling, red admiral, large and small white, meadow brown, common blue, small copper and six spot burnet are regularly recorded, the latter sometimes in thousands. In recent years, grey seals have become quite numerous in this part of Morecambe Bay and although their regular haul out is the spit at South Walney, Foulney provides the best view point, particularly in June and July. Other interesting offshore sightings observed from Foulney have included porpoise and basking shark. Voles and shrews make their home in the long grassland at the western end of the island and keep active throughout the year.

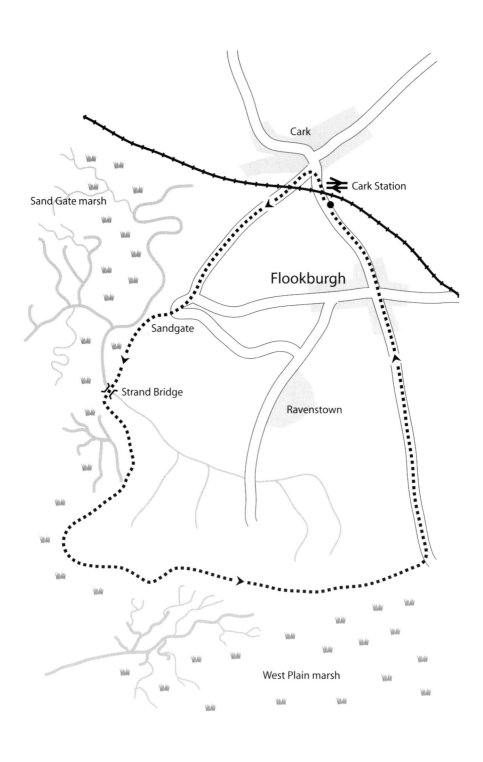

Cark

Cark Station

Sand Gate marsh

Flookburgh

Sandgate

Strand Bridge

Ravenstown

West Plain marsh

Flookborough, Sandgate and West Plain marsh

Shelduck

Start:	Starts and finishes at the Cark and Cartmel railway station
Grid Ref:	SD365762
Distance:	5 miles (8 km)
Time:	Allow four to five hours
Grade:	Easy
General:	Toilets, refreshments and shops in Grange-over-Sands (PT)

T HIS WALK TAKES IN ONE OF the larger wader roosts on Morecambe Bay and is best undertaken between mid September and mid March. To enjoy this spectacle it is essential to get the right height of tide and to plan to arrive on the coastal path at the back of West Plain marsh at least 30 minutes before high tide. The tide should be at least 9.5 metres (Liverpool height). Remember also that the tide is around fifteen minutes behind the predicted Liverpool or Morecambe time. This rather restricts the suitable days, but it is well worth planning to do the walk on such days for on lower tides the main wader roost is on the sand flats well out from the salt marsh. If doing the walk on a lower tide it is probably best to concentrate on the Sandgate marsh area, watching the wildfowl and waders assemble. The route follows the Cumbria Coastal Way for much of the time.

The walk starts at the Cark and Cartmel railway station. Turn right out of the station to pick up the signposted Cumbria Coastal Way, walking for a short distance on the road before turning left

onto a footpath across fields before another stretch of road at Sandgate Farm. If travelling by car it is recommended to park in the signed car park in the centre of Flookborough village. Proceed down the main street towards Sandgate Farm to pick up the Cumbria Coastal Way.

ⓘ This first section features mainly farmland birds including flocks of lapwing, fieldfare and redwing, the latter especially later in the winter when the berries are exhausted.

⦿ From Sandgate Farm follow the path out onto the edge of the salt marsh. From here the path hugs the edge of the marsh, following each indentation where the marsh joins the farmland. The path goes right to Cowpren Point where it picks up the old sea wall embankment.

ⓘ This section gives many good viewpoints over Sand Gate salt marsh, and as the tide flows the movement of waders towards west plain can be very impressive. These include large flocks of oystercatcher, curlew and redshank, many coming from the direction of Chapel Island. On lower tides they roost on exposed salt marsh but on the higher tides they head for West Plain marsh. Wildfowl will sit out the tide, especially on calm days, and large numbers of wigeon, shelduck, pintail and mallard congregate on the water now covering the salt marsh. Look out also for eider and red-breasted merganser, both of which have increased in recent years and the former now breeds on Chapel Island. Long-tailed duck and goosander have also occurred, while little egrets in increasing numbers have taken to searching the salt marsh creeks and pools. It is amazing how such an obvious bird can disappear completely down a creek. Watch out for them also on other sections of the walk. Check both the tide line and the fields inland for meadow pipit and, especially in winter, rock pipit and also reed bunting. The fields may support flocks of lapwing and at times golden plover, along with winter thrushes and of course the common farmland birds.

⦿ The path follows the sea wall embankment right to West Plain Farm where it rejoins the road. Take care not to leave the embankment especially on the highest of spring tides when almost all the salt marsh will be covered. Frequent stops along this section are recommended from the elevated embankment which affords excellent views.

ⓘ After turning the corner at Cowpren Point, scan the marsh immediately to check where the waders are gathering. They often start at this end of the marsh and then as the tide rises they move along the marsh towards West Plain. A good plan is to position yourself opposite the main wader concentration. These are mainly oystercatcher, curlew, knot, redshank and dunlin with smaller numbers of bar-tailed godwit and grey plover. With the tide still flowing there is constant movement, especially of the smaller waders which take to the wing as their roost site is made untenable by the rising tide. It is possible to detect when the tide is on the turn for the movement ceases, except of course if peregrine or merlin launch a sudden attack. Again it is mainly the dunlin, knot and redshank which take to the wing, the larger oystercatcher and curlew treating the attacker with disdain.

The inland fields are at their best when they are flooded following periods of heavy rain. At such times a good selection of waders feeds there, their numbers augmented at high tide by large numbers of particularly the smaller waders.

Wildfowl include numbers of shelduck, wigeon, pintail and mallard. There is also usually a gull roost, especially of the larger species. The embankment and the inland dyke and fields should be checked for reed buntings and skylarks. Water rails occasionally skulk in the overgrown dyke. At passage periods large numbers of meadow pipit and pied wagtail often pass along the salt marsh. On the seaward side the small pools and flooded areas often attract snipe, while the rushy patches occasionally hold short-eared owl, which take to the wing if flooded out by the tide.

🚶 **Follow the long straight road from West Plain Farm back to Flookborough, returning either to the car park or Cark and Cartmel railway station.**

ⓘ The road passes through mainly agricultural land and here again the fields are at their best when flooded. Numbers of oystercatcher and redshank, along with lapwing and at times golden plover, feed in the fields. They may be joined by flocks of jackdaw, and check any stubble fields for flocks of skylarks, finches and buntings.

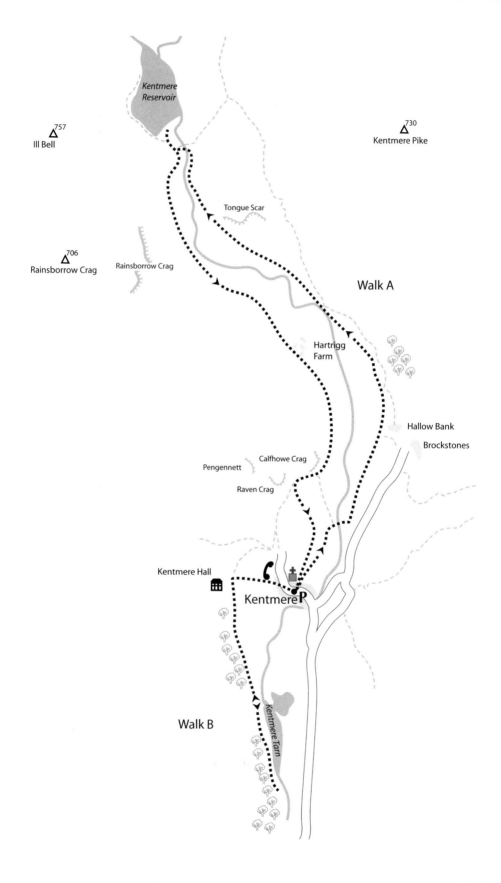

Kentmere
Reservoir

$\triangle$ 757
Ill Bell

$\triangle$ 730
Kentmere Pike

Tongue Scar

Walk A

$\triangle$ 706
Rainsborrow Crag

Rainsborrow Crag

Hartrigg
Farm

Hallow Bank

Brockstones

Calfhowe Crag

Pengennett

Raven Crag

Kentmere Hall

Kentmere P

Walk B

Kentmere Tarn

Upper Kentmere

Ring ouzel

Start: Informal car park by the village hall and church
Grid Ref: NY455041
Distance: Walk A 6.2 miles (9.9 km)
Walk B 3.2 miles (5.2 km)
Grade: Easy
General: Toilets, shops and refreshments in Staveley

THIS WALK COVERS MUCH of the upper valley of the Kent, passing through a range of habitats. Although best in the spring and summer, it gives gentle bird watching at other times of the year too. Continuous woodland is restricted to a few wooded cloughs and small plantations but much of the lower valley has many scattered groups of trees which will increase over the years due to recent widespread planting. An optional additional walk is also described (Walk B).

Walk A

From the small car park by the village hall and church take the footpath in front of the church and on past the houses at the edge of the village, then take the right-hand footpath which is signposted Mardale and Kentmere reservoir. Pass across the bridge over the river Kent, across a bracken-covered field, over a wall stile and onto a well-worn track between two walls. From there on follow the path up the valley and to the reservoir.

The noisy jackdaws nesting in the church tower are usually the first birds you see, along with house martins and swallows. Because of its scattered tree cover, Kentmere is one of the easiest places to see green woodpecker. This wonderfully colourful bird announces its presence with its loud and often repeated laughing call. If you concentrate on the area where the call comes from you will eventually get a rewarding view, often on the ground where it forages for ants and other insects. The areas around and just out of the village are the most favoured but it occurs throughout much of the valley wherever there are a few trees and seems to be commoner than its black and white cousin. In early autumn, if there is a good crop of hawthorn and mountain ash berries, flocks of redwing and fieldfare concentrate around the village.

Right from the start of the walk watch out for birds of prey. Buzzards are the commonest and although they can occur anywhere on the walk the first section is usually the most productive. Sparrowhawks also occur, again mainly in the scattered woodland areas, and peregrines are regular with several nesting pairs in the vicinity. They are present throughout year and regularly have spectacular and noisy confrontations with the ever-present ravens. The wonderful deep throaty call of the latter can be heard throughout the valley as pairs or small groups move around. Kestrels nest on the steeper rock faces and can be seen regularly hovering over the more open hillsides and fields.

Further up the valley the bracken-clothed hillsides with scattered trees and rocky outcrops are the best areas for tree pipit and whinchat. In suitable country the stonechat is easy to spot, perching upright on the top of a small bush, thistle or post flicking their tail. Pied flycatchers nest in the wooded cloughs, while redstarts are well distributed, usually preferring the more scattered groups of mature trees, and there are often excellent views of them perching on an isolated tree or stone wall. The valley is crisscrossed by stone walls, some going well up the fellside – a silent memorial to past generations of farmers and stockmen. Most are in good repair but these days many around the fertile valley floor are topped with barbed wire to keep the red deer out of the hay and silage fields. Redstarts regularly nest in holes in the walls, a habit shared with the pied wagtail.

The more open areas with less bracken and many boulders are frequented by wheatear and meadow pipit. The latter is probably the commonest breeding bird in the valley but the whole population vacates the area by late autumn, preferring the more balmy climate of southern Europe. Cuckoos still occur and the meadow pipit is its regular host. Listen for the well-known call of the male and the less well-known 'bubbling' of the female.

Wherever you get a view of the river watch out for dippers and common sandpipers. Grey wagtail also frequent the river and regularly use the smaller inflow streams. The best stretch for all these waterside birds is the last part of the river before the reservoir is reached. The reservoir was built in 1848 to supplement the water flow of the Kent which was widely used at that time to power mills in Kendal. Common sandpipers frequent the shoreline of the reservoir but other birds are only infrequent visitors, including goosander, goldeneye and tufted duck.

Cross the river by the reservoir dam and follow the well-defined track down the valley, past Hartrigg Farm where the track becomes metalled, and back to the car park.

The first part of the track passes through the now mellowed tips of earlier slate extraction. This used to be a regular area for ring ouzel but they have become less frequent in recent years. Its song, similar to but appropriately wilder than its close relative the blackbird, is the best guide in early spring, though the easiest time to get a good view is when they are feeding young in May.

Further down the valley there is much evidence of recent tree and hedge planting and the fencing-off of dyke edges. The latter has resulted in a good growth of willows and rushes and has attracted sedge warbler and reed bunting to breed.

Many of the species seen earlier on the walk also occur in similar habitat on this side of the valley. However, with its more extensive open areas together with the two large crags, it is often easier to find species such as peregrine, raven, wheatear and tree pipit.

There are many badger setts within the valley, some of them right out in the open and well away from trees. Before the bracken obscures it is possible to locate setts on the other side of the valley by scanning with binoculars for their tell-tale mounds of bare earth. Once located, a late evening visit watching from the road in early spring can give really exciting, though admittedly distant, viewing. With an overall view of the sett you can see all the comings and goings from different entrances and watch the badgers snuffle their way up the hillside, often to be followed by a quick return to the sett. On occasions five or six animals are out at once, giving you an evening to remember.

As the village is approached the tree cover increases so look out for any woodland bird you have missed. Throughout the year the green woodpecker is regular in this area. Probably the best place to see them is to look over the wall to the right just before the car park is reached. These fields with many scattered trees are a favourite area for this often elusive species. From the same viewpoint it is worth looking down the valley to the fertile fields alongside the river. In spring lapwing and redshank nest, while heron and the occasional kingfisher frequent the river

As a further option, another walk down the valley may be incorporated. This can also be a circular walk but the return is along the narrow valley road and it is recommended that this section is undertaken as an outward and return along the same route. Certainly you will see more birds this way than on the narrow and rather dangerous road.

Walk B

(ツ) **From the church take the track down the hill past a cottage, and on past Kentmere Hall Farm. Follow the left-hand track down the valley, across the bridge over the stream, passing first through woodland and out onto open fell, then again into woodland.**

❶ Kentmere Hall, with its four-storey fourteenth-century pele tower, is an impressive landmark. There is a large rookery close by and jackdaws, swallows and house martins breed in the buildings. The woodlands have many of the species you would expect in an upland wood including pied flycatcher, redstart and green and great spotted woodpecker. Treecreeper, nuthatch and long-tailed tit are also regular.

Once out into the fell area attention turns to the river and the small mere through which the river passes. This mere is the result of past extractions of diatamaceous (containing fossils) earth for use as an insulation material. Since extraction ceased the edges have become vegetated and attract breeding sedge warblers and reed buntings. Breeding water birds include tufted duck, goosander, little grebe, coot and moorhen. Kingfishers are regular visitors, while in winter goldeneye are common. The scrubby woodlands between the path and the mere attract willow warbler, whitethroat, blackcap and garden warbler.

On the open hillside tree pipits and stonechats should be looked for. Buzzard, kestrel and raven are also regular. This is another place to look out for the elusive green woodpecker, especially in open areas close to woodland.

Helsington Barrows

Woodcock

An ornithological survey

Start: National Trust car park, Helsington Barrows, Kendal
Grid Ref: SD490900
Distance: 2 miles (3.2 km)
Time: Discretionary, recommend a minimum of two hours
Grade: Easy
General: (See map on page 136.) Helsington Barrows is not conveniently served by public transport. There are no toilet or retail facilities on site. The nearest facilities are at Kendal

THIS IS AN EASY circular walk covering the varied habitat and stunning views to be had from the quaintly named Helsington Barrows. Visitors may wish to indulge in bird watching while enjoying the varied natural history of the barrows and taking in the fine views from the western ridge, which rises to a modest altitude of 212 metres.

Helsington Barrows occupies part of the carboniferous limestone escarpment of the National Trust's Sizergh Estate and forms part of the Scout and Cunswick Scar Sites of Special Scientific Interest. The Helsington site is totally enclosed by a dry stone wall, with adequate exits out onto Scout Scar proper, and the adjoining road. Limestone paving usually supports an interesting flora and this is certainly the case at Helsington Barrows, the orchid family being well represented here with dark red helleborine, fragrant and fly orchid. Yew is of great importance to the visiting flocks of finches and thrushes in the autumn when a colourful mixture of the berries of hips, rowan, hawthorn, guelder rose and elder contrast with the shades of several different species of fungi. Stands of Juniper bushes, disappearing from many localities, are still quite abundant here and contain many mature specimens.

🚶 To arrive at Helsington Barrows from the south take the minor
road left just south of the Prizet filling station on the A591 (T) and
proceed to a T-junction. Turn right on the Kendal to Brigsteer
road and the small National Trust car park is on the left.
Commence walking from the car park by following the path to
the north, eventually reaching a wall. Turn left and walk uphill
through groves of larch, yew and oak to reach the northern
corner. Turn left to join a wall situated at the western extremity
of the site and follow the wall south. At its southern end the
limestone eminence is much more exposed. This is the finest
vantage point to view the Lyth Valley and Morecambe Bay. To the
north west the more extensive limestone outcrop that is Scout
Scar unfolds to give a panoramic view of Lakeland's southern
mountains. If the weather and visibility are both good this is the
perfect place to have your picnic lunch.

🚶 Where the ground drops sharply away take the path to the left
and follow around the hillside, skirting a fallen oak tree on the
right. On reaching the trees again turn left up the valley and
continue until the west wall is almost reached. Here turn right
up the slope to reach an old hut. Continue on over the rise to
eventually regain the outward route and return to the car park.
The above circular walk covers the varied habitat of the site and
offers the best bird watching potential. Alternatively, choose any
permutation; the time taken and choice of route is yours.

ℹ The strength of the habitat for birds lies in its assemblage of tree
and shrub cover, with clumps of yew, oak and larch being especially
important. The commonest all-year round resident to look out for here
is the chaffinch, especially during the summer months. Numbers tend
to decline during the autumn as some winter dispersal takes place.
Other resident finches include the strikingly coloured bullfinch and
the equally bright goldfinch and greenfinch. Robins are common and
rigorously defend their territories throughout the year.

The green woodpecker is a common resident usually seen close to
woodland or while foraging on grassland anthills. Juveniles are seen
in most years. Great spotted woodpeckers also breed, so look and
listen out for both these two species of woodpecker. Both have an easy
bounding flight and may be seen alighting on a trunk or bough. The
green woodpecker does not drum as often as its smaller relatives the
great spotted and lesser-spotted woodpecker, though the latter species
is regarded as rare and unlikely to be encountered on the barrows.

Since 1993 the resident nuthatch population has gradually increased in deciduous woodland and expanded its range into the larch plantations. Treecreepers are common in the well-wooded areas and are particularly visible in the autumn. Large areas of bracken are found on the deeper acidic soils between limestone outcrops and this habitat supported a breeding population of yellowhammers throughout the 1990s. Site-faithful residents include jay, wood pigeon, wren, dunnock, blackbird, song and mistle thrushes, goldcrest, coal, blue and great tits and the declining marsh tit and skylark. Like other members of the tit family the marsh tit has a range of vocal utterances but listen out for the distinctive 'chick-a-bee-bee' call. The absence of the nape patch distinguishes it at once from the similar more abundant coal tit.

Ravens are normally seen or heard flying overhead, particularly in the period November to February. The buzzard and kestrel are both common resident birds of prey. Nowadays, sparrowhawk and peregrine falcon are also regularly seen. The recovery of these species has not been universally welcomed, however, and some observers see them as a threat to local bird populations. However, the available scientific evidence does not support these theories and conversely there are those who argue that we should welcome the sparrowhawk into our gardens as a sign of a healthy environment.*

Summer visitors include the commonest warbler of Helsington, the willow warbler. They should be listened for from their arrival in mid April and remain throughout the season before departure in September. The attendance of other species of warbler can be somewhat unpredictable but chiffchaff, blackcap and garden warbler are possible and should be looked and listened for wherever there is sufficient cover. The spotted flycatcher is an example of a declining summer visitor to the barrows and any sightings these days are noteworthy, August being the best month.

In late April and May the ever-perceptive observer may hear a rather thin but short song that ends rather abruptly, as high up in the green foliage the male redstart sings its little ditty. In many of its habits the redstart shows its affinity to the closely related robin. In its choice of nesting site the redstart is more restrictive than the robin and usually nests in holes of mature trees and the walls lining the barrows.

The tree pipit is now a scarce summer visitor despite the eminently suitable habitat of scattered trees and grassland to be found at the barrows. The very similar meadow pipit is both a regular summer visitor and a passage migrant, and confusion is likely for here there is

---

*   In scientific nomenclature this is known as 'population dynamics'.

an overlap of suitable habitat. However, the song of the tree pipit is far superior to that of the meadow and is delivered from the topmost branches of a tree or while descending in a parachute flight, often to the same perch, whereas the meadow pipit makes a similar but less spectacular aerial flight from the ground. The smaller meadow pipit is a host species of the cuckoo. Sadly, the cuckoo is one of a number of long-distance migrants that has declined by more than 50% in the United Kingdom during the past twenty-five years, and this is reflected at Helsington Barrows where occurrences are now far less regular. A contributing factor is that the cuckoo relies on an abundant supply of caterpillars to feed their young but the recent tendency towards prolonged periods of warm weather in springtime means that caterpillars are emerging earlier and thus there is a disparity in timing.

Flocks of fieldfare and redwing are common winter visitors and passage migrants. Undoubtedly the attraction of the barrows for these and other members of the thrush family is the annual abundant yew fruit crop. Large flocks of both species arrive in early October and quickly settle to feed, with numbers gradually decreasing by the end of December. During March and April numbers again build up prior to their departure to distant northern climes. The brambling is an interesting and attractive winter visitor, sometimes seen when large numbers irrupt from Scandinavian countries.

When the berry crop fails in Scandinavia flocks of waxwing invade Britain in search of food. During a good waxwing winter flocks may be seen in northern England and irruptions have occurred on the barrows in recent years. The crossbill has been infrequently recorded in recent years, including a flock of thirty-five which came down from the larch grove to drink. The handsome great grey shrike is a rare winter visitor to the barrows as well as to the nearby Lyth Valley. Woodcocks usually occur in winter, and in early spring may be heard and seen during the twilight hours flying over the woodlands while engaged in their roding display flight.

Examples of occasional visitors occurring at the barrows are various common warblers, lesser redpoll, pied flycatcher, osprey, red kite, ring ouzel and oystercatcher. During spring and summer swifts and swallows are commonly seen flying over the barrows but do not nest, and are categorised as both summer visitors and passage migrants. In September swallows embark on a long journey south of the Sahara to be absorbed in the scattered trees, grasslands and acacias of the African plain.

In his ornithological report completed in the year 2000, Gordon Clark – no stranger to the continent of Africa – describes the status of the ninety species of birds he encountered in his study area of Helsington Barrow. The list comprises twenty-eight residents, twenty-two summer visitors, four winter visitors, eight passage migrants and twenty-eight irruptive, vagrant and occasional species. A decade on and several species are no longer to be described as common and others such as the yellowhammer have disappeared altogether. While there are gains such as buzzard, sparrowhawk, nuthatch and bullfinch, that have increased both nationally and locally, there are plenty of other birds that have gone completely or are rapidly disappearing from the barrows, including such iconic species as the tree pipit, wood warbler, cuckoo, lapwing and curlew.

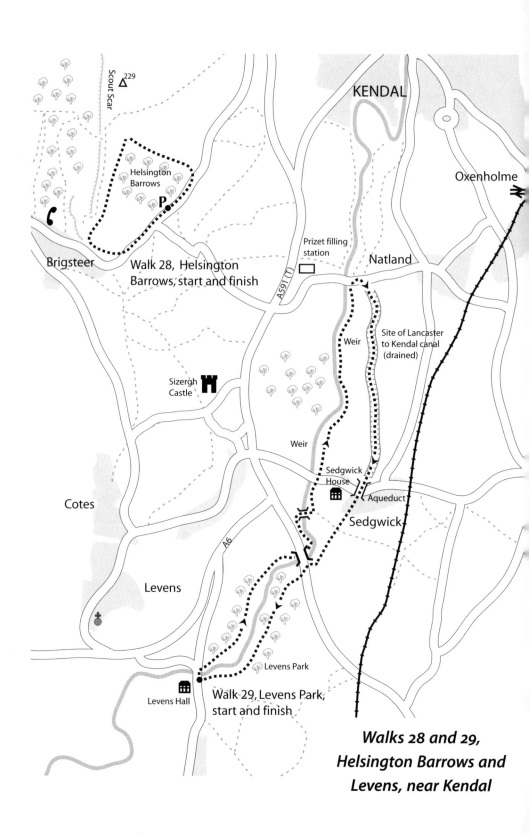

Scout Scar △²²⁹

KENDAL

Oxenholme

Helsington
Barrows

P

Brigsteer

Walk 28, Helsington
Barrows, start and finish

Prizet filling
station

Natland

A591 (T)

Weir

Site of Lancaster
to Kendal canal
(drained)

Sizergh
Castle

Weir

Cotes

A6

Sedgwick
House

Aqueduct

Sedgwick

Levens

Levens Park

Levens Hall

Walk 29, Levens Park,
start and finish

Walks 28 and 29,
Helsington Barrows and
Levens, near Kendal

Levens Park and the two waterways circular

Kingfisher

Start: Levens Bridge on the A6
Grid Ref: SD497853
Distance: 6 miles (9.7 km)
Time: Allow four to five hours
Grade: Easy
General: Refreshments, toilet and parking facilities at Natland. Levens Hall is open to the public and facilities are provided for paying visitors

THIS WALK IS ENCHANTING throughout the seasons, especially in autumn when the russet brown, flame red and yellow tints of native and exotic trees grace the Elizabethan deer park. The historic setting is further enhanced by the placid waters of the River Kent and Levens Hall, which all adds up to an overall air of serenity. On the outward route the path firstly follows the north bank of the River Kent, through Levens Park and beyond to the farthest point of the walk at Natland. The return route is via the northernmost section of the Lancaster Canal, which ran from Preston to Kendal, albeit this section is drained and filled in. The last section of the canal to Kendal opened in stages during 1818–19 and the single-arch stone Sedgwick aqueduct that forms part of the walk remains as testament to a form of transport that was eventually superseded by rail and road.

🚶 **At Levens Bridge (A6) commence the walk by taking the footpath indicated 'park head' on the north side of the bridge. The path broadly parallels the River Kent before exiting Levens Park.**

Continue to follow the way-marked route across open ground to a
road junction. Turn right onto the road and after passing under
the A590T continue to another road junction on the outskirts of
Sedgwick. Regain the south side of the river by keeping left along
the road and then proceeding left along a bridleway. Keep left
along the riverbank to a road bridge on the outskirts of Natland.
Turn right onto the road and after a short distance turn right onto
the towpath of the drained Kendal canal. Walk south along the
old towpath to a point just beyond a large skew bridge aqueduct
spanning the road in the centre of Sedgwick. Cross over the
A590T and shortly thereafter turn right to re-enter Levens Park.
The final stretch of the walk along the south side of the River
Kent completes the circular walk.

❶ Commence the walk through Levens Park. The celebrated French
landscape designer Monsieur Guillame Beaumont, who was also
responsible for the well-known topiary garden at Levens Hall, laid out
the park in the seventeenth century. A unique herd of fallow deer can
easily be overlooked and occur anywhere in the park, though they are
of course more active in late September or early October when the
rut begins. The dark Scandinavian race is probably descended from
Norman and Roman hunting stock, which preceded the more usual
spotted fallow deer.

In late winter and early spring a lone mistle thrush typically lives
up to its country name of storm cock, as it valiantly defies the March
winds and April showers. Throughout the park a few pairs of starling
and nuthatch compete for suitable tree holes to raise their families;
opportunistic stock dove and goosander, both regular visitors, may do
likewise. A more exciting prospect is the lesser spotted woodpecker,
though finding this rare and elusive species in this particular old haunt
would be rather like discovering the Holy Grail.

The River Kent, whose source lies above Kentmere, is a trout river
that is popular with anglers as well as competing heron, goosander
and in winter, goldeneye. While walking through the park, or indeed
anywhere on the river section of this walk, listen and look for the
turquoise and blue back of the resident kingfisher flying close to the
surface of the water, where sand martins nest in suitable banks. This is
a river of contrasts and upstream it is more like a brawling mountain
torrent, especially so where it cascades over Sedgwick falls, an
obstruction to migrating salmon but a haunt of grey wagtail and dipper.

Two of the hallmarks of bird watching are patience and
concentration, so listen, watch and wait for a while to be in with a

chance of seeing a flash of the grey and yellow plumage of the grey wagtail as it characteristically perches on rocks while constantly flicking its long tail. On hearing the 'zit zit zit' call of the dipper you may be lucky to see this aptly named semi-aquatic bird bobbing about or submerging into the swiftly flowing river. Nature has decreed that this rotund species should be highly specialised and thus it is quite capable of moving under water by using its wings to feed on the larvae of aquatic insects and other small invertebrates. Another clue to the presence of the dipper is the sweet song that may be heard as early as December, mingling with the sound of the tumbling water in this, its natural habitat.

After the brief interruption of a metalled road, the river and footpath draw closer together, accompanied by strips of woodland. In early spring look out for the first butterflies of the season, usually represented by the colourful peacock and small tortoiseshell butterfly. A chance encounter with a dash of lemon and yellow across a woodland clearing suggests a sighting of another early riser, the brimstone butterfly; cherish the moment and make the most of the sustainable populations of this and other species of butterflies that add a touch of glamour to the countryside.

The established large gardens fronting the river should be discreetly observed for a chance sighting of a spotted flycatcher constantly flying from a convenient perch and performing complex manoeuvres in their pursuit of flying insects. Just before you leave the River Kent at Natland look out for the convenient seat overlooking the river. This is an ideal place for a spot of lunch, so out with the sandwiches and start watching the river – I am sure that you know there is no respite when bird watching! Here, common sandpipers can be seen in their characteristic posture perched on stones in the river or making brief flights, calling attractively as they go. During springtime its call is likely to be complemented by a mixed chorus of singing willow warbler, blackcap and chiffchaff, as well as the ongoing possibilities of kingfisher, dipper and grey wagtail.

After lunch start walking along the towpath of the former Preston to Kendal canal. Under the terms of the Transport Act (1955) the 5.75 miles north of Stainton were drained and the last two miles from Crow Park Bridge to Kendal were filled in. The extant watered section between Stainmore and Tewitfield Locks is culverted by the M6 in five places but remains an interesting wildlife habitat. Venturing further south along the towpath you pass under a canal bridge, surprisingly set in splendid isolation in the middle of a field, a legacy to an age when the countryside played host to a richer variety of wildlife.

In more open country there is still a chance of seeing the curlew, with its long down-curved bill, flying over these lowland fields evocatively calling out its name. Sadly, melodic skylarks no longer ascend on quivering wings and descend like a stone into these improved grasslands of uniform green. Meanwhile expect to see omnipresent flocks of jackdaw and carrion crows, together with rooks and perhaps a few common, lesser black-back and black-headed gulls which all haunt these fields from time to time.

The woods at Larkrigg Springs are the haunt of resident nuthatch, treecreeper, great spotted woodpecker and long-tailed tits. There is often a period of overlap between the arrival of the first chiffchaffs, willow warblers and blackcaps and the migrating flocks of fieldfares and redwings trailing away in small parties to stock up on copious supplies of berries prior to returning to their Scandinavian origins. Thereafter, the towpath crosses over the spectacular Sedgwick aqueduct that spans the village street and from where the usual village suspects (birds) should be carefully looked down upon!

From the edge of Levens Park comes the crowing of a cock pheasant resplendent in its handsome and colourful plumage. Shortly thereafter the path re-enters the park and passes through a mile-long avenue of indigenous oak, beech and lime trees. This splendid feature and the lovely river setting certainly rally conservationists to the park's defence whenever planners threaten it. In wintertime during a good 'brambling winter' there is the possibility of seeing a brambling in these trees, along with flocks of chaffinch, the former picked out by its white rump and distinctive call. Typical parkland birds such as blackbird, song thrush, jay, treecreeper, nuthatch, great spotted and occasionally green woodpecker all occur on both sides of the river. Finally, on balmy summer evenings mixed flocks of swifts and hirundines turn out in force, flying low over still waters to gorge themselves on a diet of insects, perhaps a fitting conclusion to a good day's bird watching.

Whitbarrow and the Witherslack Woods

Silver washed fritillary

Start:	Start at the small informal car park near Witherslack Hall School
Grid Ref:	SD438861
Distance:	6 km (3.7 miles)
Grade:	Easy to moderate
General:	Toilets refreshments and shops at Grange-over-Sands

T HIS WALK IS DOMINATED BY the impressive limestone outcrop of Whitbarrow Scar. It offers a wide range of natural history interests as well as birds, especially plants and butterflies. A maze of paths gives access to all parts of this extensive area. It is quite possible to spend the whole day exploring this rich habitat and a leaflet with a map showing all the footpaths can be downloaded from www.limestone-pavements.org.uk.

The walk is of moderate length and covers both the woodlands at the base of the escarpment and the open habitats on top of the scar.

Park in the small informal car park by Witherslack Hall School. From here the footpath crosses a field before turning left onto the permissive path that leads through the woodlands at the base of the hill. Follow this path looking out for a right turn signposted Bell Rake and Whitbarrow. However, before taking this path make a detour along the path signposted North Lodge and bear right after 50 yards into Howe Ridding Wood, then returning along the same path and making the steep ascent onto the top of the scar.

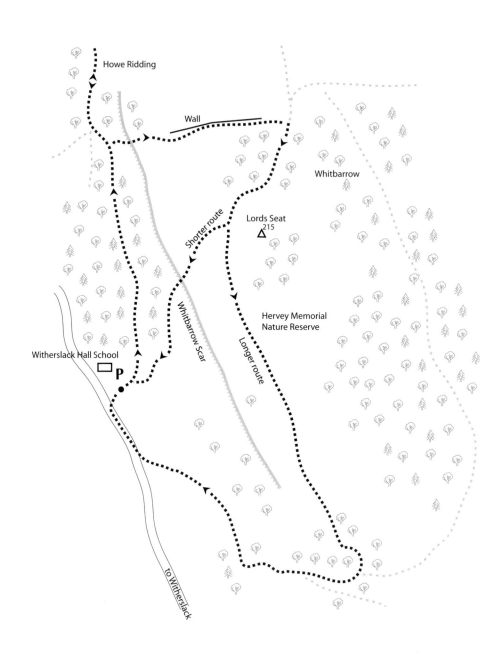

Howe Ridding

Wall

Whitbarrow

Shorter route

Lords Seat
215

Whitbarrow Scar

Hervey Memorial
Nature Reserve

Longer route

Witherslack Hall School

P

to Witherslack

❶ Even from the car park the views of the scar are impressive and straight away give an impression of the size of the site. Whitbarrow means 'white hill' and first views confirm this very fitting title. The cliffs are home to a well-known pair of peregrines and a scan of the cliffs usually reveals at least one bird. A notice on the gate banning climbing during the nesting season tells you straight away if they are in residence. Peregrines regularly return throughout the year to roost or just sit on the crag, so a scan of the crag is worthwhile at any time of year. The other inhabitant of the cliffs is the raven; throughout the walk it is impossible to miss the wonderfully deep raucous call of this increasing species. They patrol all areas of the site and family groups or even small flocks are sighted regularly.

The woodlands are mainly oak, birch and ash and are growing on shale, giving an interesting botanical comparison to the limestone areas higher on the scar. In spring a blue haze of bluebells, contrasting with the white of the wood anemones, clothes the woodland floor. The 'green woodpecker is a resident and is often detected by its call, but seeing one can be difficult and frustrating. However, the open areas created by coppicing give the best chance, because this species regularly feeds on the ground. Great spotted woodpecker, marsh tit, bullfinch and nuthatch are common throughout the year, while the more scrubby areas with good bramble growth support blackcap, garden warbler and chiffchaff during the spring and summer. The path may be muddy in places but it gives a good opportunity to check out the mammal population by looking for tracks; roe deer and badger are the most regular, but red deer also occur.

Coppicing of the hazel scrub layer is the main management here. This is done to provide ideal conditions for butterflies and is carried out on a rotational basis. Violets are the food plant of the caterpillars of the five species of fritillary butterfly which occur here in good numbers and there is an impressive flush of violets immediately after coppicing. Each butterfly has its own flight periods, starting with the pearl-bordered fritillary in May and ending with the silver washed in July and early August. However, on a warm sunny day in July it is quite possible to have the delight of seeing four species of fritillary in flight on the same day, with small pearl-bordered, dark green, high brown and the most impressive of all the silver washed on the wing. The abundant blackberry flower and thistles provide the essential nectar. The sixth fritillary, the Duke of Burgundy, is not a true fritillary but is in the metalmark family; its caterpillars feed on cowslips and primroses and it flies in June. Howe Ridding Wood is the best area for butterflies, with plenty of nectar sources throughout the season to attract a wide range of species. The butterfly of the woodlands though is the speckled wood, now abundant having colonised the area over the past thirty years.

🕺 **Take the path signposted Bell Rake and Whitbarrow. Once on top of the escarpment there is a wide range of footpaths allowing walks of varying lengths, but there is only one way down to return to the car park. The best and longest walk follows a wide circle and takes in much of the Whitbarrow Nature Reserve before swinging back to the path down the escarpment.**

🛈 Watch out for redstart and redpoll among the scattered trees and woodland edge on the incline. Once on top of the escarpment, the open grassland with scattered trees and rocky outcrops supports breeding skylark, meadow pipit, wheatear and tree pipit, with whitethroat and linnet in the more scrubby parts. Cuckoos used to be common but as in most other places they have declined, with just a few hanging on. Green woodpeckers regularly hunt ants on the grassland areas and in this habitat gives the best hope of prolonged views. Buzzards, which breed in the valley woodlands, regularly soar over the escarpment, usually singly or in pairs but on occasions larger numbers may be seen, often disputing with ravens or carrion crows. The other woodland bird of prey, the sparrowhawk, also ventures out onto the more open areas at times, flying low and using any available cover to surprise its intended victim. Peregrines and kestrels also regularly hunt the area.

The rich limestone flora includes wild daffodil and primrose in the woodlands in spring, and birds foot trefoil, thyme, rock rose, carline thistle and dropwort on the grassland. The grassland is dominated by the blue moor grass with the distinctive springtime flowers from which it takes its name. While common here it is rare elsewhere in Britain. The commonest shrub in this area is the juniper. The limestone pavement and scree are the best areas for ferns, including rigid buckler fern. The rare, dark-red helliborine occurs here along with fly and bee orchids. Butterflies of this area include common blue, wall, grayling and small heath.

🕺 **The way down the escarpment is marked by the aptly named Lord's Seat and passes down the escarpment woodland, past the mown football field and out onto the field and then back to the car park.**

❶ Back in woodland, dominated here by wind-pruned yew, there is a chance to catch up with any species you have missed. As you descend, the gaps in the trees allow a good view over the woodland, sometimes giving eye-level views of hunting peregrine or buzzard. The area around the football field has a good growth of thistles and knapweed – ideal for attracting the fritillaries, giving close views of the all-important underwing and allowing you to work out which species are present.

Other titles in the Birdwatching Walks series

available at www.carnegiepublishing.com,
on 01524 840111 or from all good bookshops

Birdwatching walks in the Yorkshire Dales

by Brendan Threfall

The Yorkshire Dales is an enchantingly beautiful area in the heart of northern England. It is a land of limestone pavements and scars, fast-flowing rivers and dramatic waterfalls, lonely heather moors and picturesque villages and valleys. But as well as its wonderful landscapes, the Dales is also a special place for many bird species, and these twin assets are combined in this excellent new book. Each of these well designed walks is set in gorgeous countryside where there is also every chance of seeing some of the birds which abounds in the area. Both novice and experienced birders can enjoy the dippers at Aysgarth, or great spotted woodpeckers in Grass Woods, as well as the rarer black grouse, wood warbler, pied flycatcher and nightjar, to name but a few.

With helpful guide maps, interesting bird and habitat information, travel hints and a bird reference section, Birdwatching walks in the Yorkshire Dales should ensure that walkers of all abilities really can get the best out of this stunning National Park and its rich and varied bird population.

ISBN: 978-1-874181-53-8
Pages: 192
Page size: 234 × 156 mm
Illustrations: maps and colour illustrations
Price: £7.95

Birdwatching walks around Morecambe Bay

by John Wilson and David Hindle

Morecambe Bay is an amazing place. Set against the magical backdrop of the Lakeland fells, it is an ever-changing world of water and sand moulded by the constant ebb and flow of the tides, a beautiful landscape in which to walk, and home to one of the largest concentrations of birds in Europe.

Tens of thousands of waders, wildfowl and gulls winter or breed, or pass through on their migrations from the Arctic to Africa and beyond, making it an area of truly national and international importance.

This book, with forty specially chosen walks, covers Morecambe Bay, from the Wyre estuary in the south to Walney Island in the north, embraces the neighbouring Duddon estuary and the peripheral areas of the southern Lake District and Forest of Bowland. It describes where and when to find the birds and other wildlife in this unique area.

ISBN: 978-1-874181-37-8
Pages: 192
Page size: 234 × 156 mm
Illustrations: *maps and colour illustrations*
Price: £7.95

This excellent book is perfect for anyone wishing to combine a love of walking with an interest in birds and other wildlife and is one of our best selling walking books.

Birdwatching walks in Bowland

by David Hindle and John Wilson

The Forest of Bowland is a truly stunning and immensely important Area of Outstanding Natural Beauty. Many species of birds – some of them rare – are there to be enjoyed within the varied habitats of the Bowland landscape, a fact that is celebrated to the full in this superb new book.

Over 30 scenic walks cover the whole of the area, from Lancaster to Pendle, and from Preston to Settle, each one designed to give the walker the chance to encounter a wide range of different birdlife in a magnificent Bowland setting.

`The authors clearly know their area and their subject – the descriptions of the landscape, its bird life and the detailed routes to follow make this one of the best guide books I have come across.'
Garstang Courier

'The sheer variety of birds to be found in the Bowland area is quite remarkable and with this book it should be made a somewhat more pleasurable experience trying to observe them … the site descriptions are concise and informative, while the bird information is refreshingly far from over-optimistic … No outdoors enthusiast should be without a copy of this fine guide.'
Lancaster Guardian

ISBN: 978-1-874181-40-8
Pages: 192
Page size: 234 × 156 mm
Illustrations: maps and colour illustrations
Price: £7.95